Sigmund Freud's Inner Divisions

Sigmund Freud's Inner Divisions shows how the limits of Freud's theory are linked to his inner conflicts, particularly those relating to his father.

Ken Fuchsman undertakes a close reading of how what Freud wrote during self-analysis reflected his inner personal divisions. This book explores how Freud's psychological divisions led to intellectual contradictions in his psychoanalytic doctrines, showing that the limits of his theory are rooted in inner conflicts that prevented his science of the unconscious from being truly comprehensive. It also considers how Freud's ideas were shaped by his internal struggles, discoveries, and denials, revealing how these inner tensions permeated his psychoanalytic theories on experience, science, civilization's higher achievements, love, and even the Oedipus complex itself.

Sigmund Freud's Inner Divisions will be of great interest to psychoanalysts in practice and in training, and to academics and scholars of the history of psychology, psychobiography, and intellectual history.

Ken Fuchsman is Emeritus faculty from the University of Connecticut, where he taught American history, interdisciplinary studies, the nature of being human, and the family in interdisciplinary perspective, and was Executive Programme Director of the Bachelor of General Studies Programme. Along with Michael Maccoby, Dr Fuchsman co-edited *Psychoanalytic and Historical Perspectives on the Leadership of Donald Trump* (Routledge).

History of Psychoanalysis
Series Editor Peter L. Rudnytsky

This series seeks to present outstanding new books that illuminate any aspect of the history of psychoanalysis from its earliest days to the present, and to reintroduce classic texts to contemporary readers.

Other titles in the series:

Sigmund Freud and his Patient Margarethe Csonka
A Case of Homosexuality in a Woman in Modern Vienna
Michal Shapira

Sigmund Freud, 1856–1939
A Biographical Compendium
Christfried Toegel

The Marquis de Puysegur and Artificial Somnambulism
Memoirs to Contribute to the History and Establishment of Animal Magnetism
Edited and translated by Adam Crabtree and Sarah Osei-Bonsu

The Subversive Edge of Psychoanalysis
David James Fisher

Freud's British Family
Reclaiming Lost Lives in Manchester and London
Roger Willoughby

Sigmund Freud's Inner Divisions
Personal and Theoretical
Ken Fuchsman

For further information about this series please visit https://www.routledge.com/ The-History-of-Psychoanalysis-Series/book-series/KARNHIPSY

Sigmund Freud's Inner Divisions

Personal and Theoretical
[1]

Ken Fuchsman

Routledge
Taylor & Francis Group

LONDON AND NEW YORK

Designed cover image: © Melanie George

First published 2026
by Routledge
4 Park Square, Milton Park, Abingdon, Oxon OX14 4RN

and by Routledge
605 Third Avenue, New York, NY 10158

Routledge is an imprint of the Taylor & Francis Group, an informa business

© 2026 Ken Fuchsman

For Product Safety Concerns and Information please contact our EU representative GPSR@taylorandfrancis.com. Taylor & Francis Verlag GmbH, Kaufingerstraße 24, 80331 München, Germany.

Trademark notice: Product or corporate names may be trademarks or registered trademarks, and are used only for identification and explanation without intent to infringe.

British Library Cataloguing-in-Publication Data
A catalogue record for this book is available from the British Library

ISBN: 9781041074700 (hbk)
ISBN: 9781041074694 (pbk)
ISBN: 9781041074717 (ebk)

DOI: 10.4324/9781041074717

Typeset in Times New Roman
by codeMantra

Contents

Acknowledgments   *viii*

Introduction   1

PART I   7

1   Freud and Fathers: Sigmund Freud's Inner Struggles   9

2   Fathers and Sons: Freud's Discovery of the Oedipus Complex   24

3   The Evolution of Freud's View of Parental/Paternal Authority   38

4   Freud and the Vienna Psychoanalytic Society   43

PART II   51

5   Biology and Experience in Freud's Thought   53

6   Freud, Psychoanalysis, and Science   63

7   Civilization's Achievement and Freudian Psychoanalysis   71

8   The Freudian Psychology of Love   80

9   What Does Freud Mean by the Oedipus Complex?   88

Index   *109*

Acknowledgments

The following articles are reprinted with permission of the publishers:

What Does Freud Mean by the Oedipus Complex. *Free Associations,* 2001, Volume Nine, Part One, Number 49.

Fathers and Sons: Freud's Discovery of the Oedipus Complex, *Psychoanalysis and History,* 2004, Vol. 6 No. 1.

Freud's Leadership and Viennese Psychoanalysis, *Clio's Psyche,* 2006, Volume 13, Number 1.

The Freudian Psychology of Love, *Clio's Psyche,* 2009, Volume 15, Number 4.

Greatness and Paradox: Sigmund Freud in the 1890s and Beyond, *Movies, Rock & Roll, Freud.* 2021. ORI Academic Press.

Introduction

In 2002, the academic platform Research Gate sought to determine the most influential psychologists. In both journal citations and introductory psychology books, Sigmund Freud was far and away number one (Research Gate, 2002). Not only that, in 2017 among the living and dead Freud was also the most cited of all scientists (Morley, 2017).

What are we to conclude? Sigmund Freud, more than 80 years after his death, remains a cultural and intellectual influence of the first rank. He has been written about extensively by psychologists, philosophers, novelists, literary critics, anthropologists, among others. His own work has had major impacts on painters and film directors.

This Viennese physician and psychoanalyst upset the human apple cart. His revolutionary doctrines reshaped our self-concept. His ambitious aim was to establish psychoanalysis as a science of the unconscious. The field's focus is on what is below the psychological surface that is mentally, emotionally, and sexually complex. Yet his movement has aroused furious criticism, eloquent advocates, and competing factions from his day unto ours. How can we assess the merits of his psychoanalytic doctrines? This evaluation has been ongoing for over a 100 years. It has sometimes been called the Freud wars.

I enter this controversial fray. My focus is to examine both the personal roots of Freud's discoveries and to evaluate if he has produced a comprehensive science of the unconscious. The first part of my approach adheres to a certain perspective. As English professor and psychoanalyst Peter Rudnytsky writes, "the achievements of creative thinkers and writers have roots in the soil of personal experience" (Rudnytsky, 2011, p. xxiv). Psychoanalyst and psychobiographer James Anderson recommends that when "we study the connection between psychologists (or psychoanalysts') life and work, we especially want to see the relevance of their personal experience to their chief concepts" (Anderson 2024, p. 20). I am clearly in the same camp as Rudnytsky and Anderson. I seek to achieve this result through a close reading of Freud's texts in public publications and personal letters. It remains important to assess Freud's work. Despite all that has been written about him, there are still additional ways of understanding Freud's creations and person.

DOI: 10.4324/9781041074717-1

How so? There are two central themes in this book: the personal and the theoretical. In the first part, I show his internal struggles and triumphs in the last four years of the 19th century. Second, I demonstrate how the divisions he had psychologically impacted on his theoretical writings. This does not much dwell on what has made Freud so prominent and influential. It one-sidedly centers on what both psychologically and intellectually kept him from developing a full account of human psychology. Another book would be needed to do justice to the revolutionary sides of his remarkable theories.

In the first chapter, I detail how, between 1896 and 1897, Freud made remarkable assertions, revolutionary discoveries, and reversed himself a number of times. Much of this transpired during his early self-analysis. In this period, Freud had pronounced psychological struggles. This became evident following the publication of his 1896 articles on the seduction theory and his father's death that year. These essays on hysteria revealed empirical findings of multiple cases. Among these clients, multiple categories of persons were identified as sexual perverts with children. Then from the winter through the summer of 1897, Freud changed direction. In letters, he accused fathers, including his own, of being the primary perpetrator who sexually abused their own children. Sigmund Freud specified that his father, Jakob, was the main cause of the neurosis of his brother and several sisters. When Freud in August 1897, diagnosed himself as having a little hysteria, it likely crossed his mind that what caused his psychological disorder had also infected some of his siblings.

On September 21, 1897, Freud dramatically reversed course again. No longer was actual childhood sexual exploitation the center of his thought. He proclaimed it was childhood fantasies more than actual abuses that were at play (Freud, 1985, pp. 264–266). This letter was the major turning point in his development. It set the stage for multiple other elaborations of the role of fantasy and the unconscious. Following this letter, Freud found ways of acquitting his own dad of abusing him. He followed this by originating the Oedipus complex. This doctrine switched gears from blaming perverted fathers to desiring sons. The drama about his own father and hysteria culminated in discounting actual experience and focusing on the unconscious. His internal divisions about fathers appeared to be diminished, but they were not. Freud wrote about his ambivalences about Jakob Freud for the rest of his life.

One example: Freud, in 1924, made admissions about his family dynamics as a child that undercut his conception of the Oedipus complex as a triangle between mother, father, and child. In a significant footnote, he found that someone else had replaced his father as rival for his beloved mother (Freud, 1960 [1901], SE VI, p. 51). This is discussed in the book's second chapter. As time went on, there was also an evolution in Freud's thought on parental/paternal authority. Early on, Freud declared that the progress of humanity was dependent on children becoming independent of their parents' control. This viewpoint evolved over time, and Freud became insistent on obedience to paternal authority, especially his own. This is traced in the third chapter. The next chapter is a case study on how Freud in the Vienna Psychoanalytic Society became insistent on conformity to his doctrines. He vacillated between acting like a patriarch and a competitive sibling. Unlike some other group leaders, his personality did not lend itself to obedience by all his followers. The diverse factions that appeared in the Vienna group also found other permutations among psychoanalysts during his life. The history of psychoanalysis is one of competing and conflicting factions and epistemological dilemmas. This pattern developed under Freud's command. He was not as successful at eliminating what he labeled as "heresy." Clearly, Sigmund Freud's struggles over fathers and paternal authority were evident in multiple ways.

This leads to the book's second theme. In his career from 1897 until 1939, Freud's distinction between the internal and external frequently pervaded his intellectual creations. In doing so, he narrowed the subject matter of his science of the unconscious. His discounting of how experiences, such as sexual abuse or enduring combat in war, can impact on a person's psychic reality weakened his theories. His divisions and denials are present in his doctrines. In this second part of the book, I will seek to document how Freud's inner conflicts impacted on his theoretical work.

In addition, at least two demons originating with Freud have haunted the history of psychoanalysis. One is that while Freud insisted that psychoanalysis was indeed a science, he resisted having it empirically examined by scientific standards. The fiercest indictments of Freud and psychoanalysts come from those who insist psychoanalysis is not a science.

A second demon is that from Freud's day to ours, as mentioned, psychoanalysis has been divided into different factions and schools. Diverse and conflicting doctrines have been put forth. Walls often exist between the different varieties of psychoanalysis. As some distinguished analysts have pointed out, psychoanalysis has not found criteria to adjudicate different claims. Freud's divisions and resistances set the stage for the existence of these still powerful dilemmas. Needless to say, the splitting into different factions is a common phenomenon in movements of various kinds. In psychoanalysis, this has often taken the form of not being sufficiently able to adjudicate epistemological conflicts.

These are the central themes with which I grapple with in this volume. I do so by closely reading and critically confronting written texts. As with any of us divided beings, it is in confronting and analyzing our inner conflicts that we become less self-deceptive. As well as trying to document Freud's limitations, I also hope to humanize him. The paradox of Freud was how he combined being flexible and innovative, rigid and dogmatic. He was internally both loose and often defensive.

Years ago, I came across a quote from a Michel de Montaigne's essay that hit home for me. "We are, I know not how, we are double within ourselves that we do not believe what we believe and cannot rid ourselves of what we condemn" (Montaigne, 1943, p. 570). It fits Freud, as well as most of us.

Many sons have mixed feelings about their father. But how many in the first decade of the 20th century would put in print that their father was cowardly in the face of an anti-Semitic bully. Or for that matter, tell the public that his father's death was the most poignant loss of his life. He makes these confessions not in a memoir but in an important scholarly work on dreams. That Freud would do so publicly indicates how significant issues about his own father were for his personal life. Certainly, no other comparable writers to Freud in this period such as the German Kraft-Ebbing, the French Pierre Janet, or the English Havelock Ellis made confessions about their fathers in print.

This concern about his father and fathers, in general, was present in 1913 when Freud declared that the very foundation of social psychology was about the son's relationship with his father (Freud, 1955 [1913], SE XIII, p. 157). It continued in 1936, the year Freud turned 80. He then wrote about the son's desire to surpass the father and how this was forbidden (Freud, 1964 [1936], Se XXII, p. 247). Worries about his father occupied Freud throughout his career. There are a number of components of Freud's psychoanalytic doctrines that can be illuminated by showing the relation to his own psychological dilemmas reflected in his 1897 decision to separate rather than interconnect the inner and outer.

In the second part of this book, I elucidate how Freud's psychological divisions limited the coherence and comprehensiveness of his theories. I demonstrate these problems with his discussion of the relationship between biology and experience, of psychoanalysis as a science, how the human mental structure made possible civilizations highest achievements, in his psychology of love, and in his beloved Oedipus complex.

Chapter 5 is entitled Biology and Experience in Freud's Thought. It might have appeared that Freud settled the distinction between the internal and external in September 1897, yet between 1905 and 1915 he re-opened the relationship between heredity and experience. His thinking on these subjects often moved in opposite directions at the same time. Then in 1913, Freud embraces a radical phylogenetic inheritance theory that points in just one direction. His intellectual dialectic of moving in disparate directions followed by a single path resembles the back and forth of the 1896–1897 period. That time of reversals and resolutions culminated in his placing the unconscious over and above the actual. These later Freudian ruminations ended up with the same result as earlier. Fantasy was declared to be more important than experience.

Freud's embracing the empirically discredited phylogenetic inheritance re-opens the question of the relationship of Freudian psychoanalysis to science. This is the subject matter of Chapter 6. Sigmund Freud himself viewed psychoanalysis as "the foundation for a new and deeper science of the mind which would be equally indispensable for the understanding of the normal" (Freud 1959 [1925], SE XX, p. 47). Some of Freud's critics have insisted that his formulations are more speculation than science. This skepticism of the scientific credibility of Freud's claims is the demon that has haunted psychoanalysis. Freud affirmed science but insisted on keeping psychoanalysis independent of other fields. Freud never established criteria by which psychoanalytic notions could be evaluated and tested. Sigmund Freud both affirmed the centrality of science while in practice keeping his own doctrines separate from evaluation by scientific practices and standards.

The seventh chapter returns to the relationships of the internal and external. It ultimately does so by examining Freud's 1930 declaration of the high achievements of civilization in recent times. The question becomes what in Freud's view of human mental structure can account for such advances in science, culture, and the arts. To make that analysis, Freud's perspectives on the human mental tendencies in both his topographical and structural model are discussed. This would include what he means by the reality principle, sublimation, and Eros. It turns out that insufficiencies in his explication of what would drive humans toward these higher cultural activities are shown. He assumes that humans wish to engage with these demanding mental activities. But he is never able to specify how the leap from the pleasure principle to sublimation and Eros would motivate the higher activities. Freud cannot explain why someone would be more drawn to advanced physics than being a poker expert.

In Chapter 8, given Freud's embracing Eros as the life instinct, it is worthwhile looking at what Freud says about love and sex. How Freud treats love can illuminate the connection between the inner and outer. At times, he discusses love in terms derived from his understanding of family structure and dynamics. The boy is focused on his being sexually drawn to his mother, but suffers from both the presence of the father and the birth of younger siblings. These things can lead to a narcissistic scar and the son feeling embittered by the presence of other rivals. For the daughter, Freud maintains that an adult pair bonding can never psychologically replace the father in the female psyche. Freud writes about both fulfillment in sexual relationships and that there is something in them that brings unfulfillment. To him love ends up being more about being self-concerned than containing mutuality and/or dedication to the well-being of the love partner. He focuses more on the internal than the dynamics of the love relationship itself.

The last regular chapter returns to Freud and the Oedipus complex. He revised, subtracted, and added to the central component of this psychoanalytic staple for over 40 years. He had declared that the Oedipus complex was a triad of mother-father-child that was dictated to us by nature. He never wavered from these propositions. Yet his own writings demonstrate that external factors such as family structure and dynamics can influence the shape of an individual's Oedipus complex. He discusses these dynamics in the role of siblings who become Oedipal rivals. He also assumes facts not in evidence by claiming that children are told about castration by women, but gives no evidence to support this contention. Freud also assumes that even if a child does not have a mother or father in their family that the Oedipus complex develops given the phylogenetic inheritance. Again, Freud's own divisions and ways of thinking through issues contribute to the lack of coherence in his Oedipal theory. He is confounded in the Oedipal complex by the relationship of the real and the imagined as he is in other components of his theories.

As mentioned, the conflicts within his doctrines can be traced to discoveries and denials in his September 21, 1897, letter to Fliess. His psychological divisions contributed both to his extraordinary greatness and his theoretical dilemmas. Freud is not alone in having one's inner conflicts influence their published work. Connecting Freud's psychological issues to his theoretical insufficiencies helps us understand the man and the theorist.

References

Anderson, J. (2024). *Psychobiography: In search of the inner life.* Oxford University Press.

Freud, S. (1955). *Totem and taboo. The standard edition of the complete psychological works,* SE XIII (J. Strachey Ed. and Trans.). The Hogarth Press (Original work published 1913).

Freud, S. (1959). *An autobiographical study. Standard edition,* SE XX (J. Strachey Ed. and Trans.). The Hogarth Press (Original work published 1925).

Freud, S. (1960). *The psychopathology of everyday life, Standard edition,* SE VI (J. Strachey Ed. and Trans.). The Hogarth Press (Original work published 1901).

Freud, S. (1964). *A disturbance of memory on the Acropolis. Standard edition,* SE XXII (J. Strachey Ed. and Trans.). The Hogarth Press (Original work published 1936).

Freud, S. (1985). *The complete letters of Sigmund Freud to Wilhelm Fliess, 1887–1904* (J. M. Masson Ed. and Trans.). Harvard University Press.

Montaigne, M. de (1943). *The complete works* (D. Frame Trans). Everyman's Library.

Morley, J. (2017). The World's Most Cited Scientists, (23) The World's Most Cited Scientists | LinkedIn.

Research Gate (2002). Top 60 Psychologists, Top 60 Psychologists According to Total Citation Pages in 10 Name Indexes | Download Table.

Rudnytsky, P. (2011). *Rescuing psychoanalysis from Freud: And other essays in re-vision.* Routledge.

Part I

Chapter 1

Freud and Fathers

Sigmund Freud's Inner Struggles

The "problems of social psychology," Freud asserted in 1913, "prove soluble on the basis of one single concrete point-man's relation to his father" (Freud, 1955 [1913], SE XIII, p. 157). A few years before, in the 1908 preface to the second edition of *The Interpretation of Dreams*, he said that "this book" had a "subjective significance for me personally." It was the part of "my reaction to my father's death – that is to say, to the most important event, the most poignant loss, of a man's life" (Freud, 1953 [1908], SE IV, p. xxvi). Clearly, through 1913 the issue of fathers had deep emotional resonance for Sigmund Freud. His psychological divisions about his father led him down personal and theoretical paths that were both revolutionary and self-divided.

If we turn to his letters and publications in the period just before his father's death in October 1896 through the 1900 publication of *The Interpretation of Dreams*, the actions of fathers are front and center. He goes through multiple twists and turns of much psychological significance. When he comes up with his formulation of the Oedipus complex in October 1897, he has arrived at a particular formulation that remained a foundation of his psychoanalytic doctrines. This period in the late 1890s is also the time of his intense self-analysis and what he describes as his own little hysteria.

It is worth journeying once again down this well-traveled highway and focusing mostly on Freud's shifting perspectives on the role of fathers, including his own. The tale of Sigmund Freud cannot be fully understood without seeing how his own psychological divisions over Jakob Freud influenced what he included and excluded from his doctrines.

Sigmund Freud is one of the most innovative, influential, and controversial thinkers who have ever lived. There was a dialectic in his thought that led him more than once to reject notions that were once prominent in his personal and intellectual struggles. This internal dialogue led to his psychoanalytic theories often being one sided and partial.

This chapter will trace how Sigmund Freud moved from focusing on what were portrayed as actual events to favoring the unconscious over material reality, and with his making little attempt to interconnect the real and the imagined. Though many in contemporary psychoanalytic mainstreams have left much of Freud

DOI: 10.4324/9781041074717-3

behind, his struggles, achievements, and limits can be illuminating for the challenges the psychoanalytic movement still faces.

Jakob and Sigmund, Fathers and Sons

Sigmund Freud endured an emotional and intellectual crisis following his father's 1896 death. After much switching of positions, Freud culminated this part of his journey in his great 1897 discoveries. There is a sequence in his views about fathers, which included his 1896 theories of hysteria. These assert that actual sexual abuse of children leads to this disorder. His views here interconnect the internal and external. In September 1897 and afterwards, as mentioned, he focuses less on actual perpetrators than the child's unconscious fantasies. His journey in this period goes from documenting a variety of abusers, to centering on fathers as sexual perverts, to seeing the unconscious, and then the Oedipus complex as primary.

But there were residues of these internal struggles within Freud's psyche. As Montaigne writes, "we are, I know not how, double within ourselves, with the result that we do not believe what we believe, and we cannot rid ourselves of what we condemn" (Montaigne, 1943 [1578–1580], p. 570). This statement of Montaigne's helps us understand Freud's personal and intellectual divisions throughout his career as a psychoanalyst.

As Freud moves from the seduction theory to the Oedipus complex, he sometimes argues against what he once championed. An exploration of his reversals and affirmations shows that as Freud is breaking new ground, he also leaves under addressed some of his own intellectual and personal dilemmas. In the rest of his career, he does not psychologically rid himself of what he was intent on rejecting.

A side of Freud's being human is his multi-sided responses to his father. First, he cared for him. After his father's death, Freud wrote Fliess about Jakob, "I valued him highly…and with his peculiar mixture of deep wisdom and fantastic light-heartedness he had a significant effect on my life….in [my] inner self the whole past has been reawakened by this event" (Freud, 1985, p. 202). Jakob recognized how bright Sigmund was as a child, educated his son himself, later with the family's quite limited means wanted Sigmund to attend good schools. Yet beyond these powerful kinship bonds, Sigmund harbored ambivalent attitudes toward his father. This led to lifelong struggles on Freud's part over his feelings about Jakob and the role of fathers in human psychology. It is the son's ambivalence toward Jakob and fathers, and how it influenced his theories that is the subject of what follows. It is quite a journey.

The concerns Sigmund had about his father were financial and whether Jakob was a sufficient role model. In January 1884, 27-year-old Sigmund wrote his fiancé, about Jakob and his two adult half-brothers. "Yesterday I met Father in the street, still full of projects, still hoping. I took it upon myself to write to Emanuel and Philipp urging them to help Father out of his present predicament" (Freud, 1960, p. 86). This was not a one-time worry. As biographer Louis Breger puts it, Jakob had a "lifelong inability to provide for the family" (Breger, 2000, p. 25). There was no record of Freud's father in either the Vienna Trade Register or the Trade Tax register, which means he was not a trader of any sort (Clark, 1980, p. 15). It seems that Jakob and his dependents were kept afloat by money sent him by his sons in England and his wife's family, among others (Whitebook, 2017, pp. 62–63). His family's economic struggles had a legacy for Sigmund. In his 1925 autobiography Freud mentioned "my father's generous improvidence" (Freud, 1959 [1925], SE XX, p. 10).

It was not only about money that Freud thought Jakob wanting. In the most well-known incident, Jakob tells his 10–12-year-old boy of when a Christian knocked off Jakob's hat and said Jew get off the pavement. When Sigmund asked his dad what he did, the father replied he picked his hat up. The son wrote, "This struck me as unheroic conduct." In his mind, he contrasted Carthaginian general Hannibal's heroism with Jakob's meekness (Freud, 1953 [1900], SE IV, p. 197). Sigmund sought other paternal models, while remaining uneasy over his judgment of Jakob.

To Freud, there is a "tragic guilt" that stems from "rebellion against...authority" (Freud, 1955 [1913], p. 156). He writes that "the son's sense of guilt and the son's rebelliousness...never became extinct" (Freud, 1955 [1913], p. 152). Writing in 1936, Freud again talks of "a sense of guilt" that "has something to do with a child's criticism of his father." Freud writes that "the essence of success was to have gotten further than one's father, and as though to excel one's father was still something forbidden" (Freud, 1964 [1936], SE XXII, p. 247).

A discontented Sigmund not only sought to go further than Jakob, the son expressed wishes to replace his father. Sigmund had two adult half-brothers who were old enough to be his parent. In his late teens, Sigmund visited his older half-brother, Emanuel, in England and had a fantasy "of how different things would have been if I had been born the son not of my father but of my brother" (Freud, 1960 [1901], SE VI, pp. 219–220). In 1924, he writes of himself and family when he was about three years old. He says his adult half-brother Philipp "had taken his father's place as the child's rival" (Freud, 1960 [1901], SE VI, p. 51). For decades, Sigmund vacillated between appreciating his father, being judgmental, wanting a different father, and then feeling guilty for what he thought about Jakob. Important elements of Freud's theories involve fathers and sons. Sigmund's ambivalence about his own father influenced the evolution of his theories.

When in 1896 Freud published articles on the origins of hysteria, he focused on sexual misconduct by adults and childhood siblings. Freud listed a number of possible perpetrators of sexual abuse (Freud, 1962 [1896], SE. III, p. 208). His emphasis on diverse agents initiating abuse of children began to change not long after his father's death on October 23, 1896. Less than two weeks after Jakob died, Sigmund wrote that "the old man's death has affected me deeply.... I now feel quite uprooted" (Freud, 1985, [1896], p. 202).

This being shaken up by Jakob's demise soon took some unusual paths. Just six weeks after his father died, on December 6, 1896, Sigmund wrote Fliess that "more and more" the perverse seduction that results in hysteria is "seduction by the father" (Freud, 1985, [1896], p. 212). Freudian partisan Kurt Eissler finds this alteration from many different abusers to fathers perplexing. He reports that "only two of the series of twelve women patients could possibly have been the victims of assaults by fathers" (Eissler, 2001, pp. 152–153). On Freud's journey, about fathers is where he begins to ignore his prior empirical findings. He also makes bold assertions without providing any documentation. Freud went even further. On February 8, 1897, Freud told Fliess, "My own father was one of those perverts and is responsible for the hysteria of my brother (all of whose symptoms are identifications) and those of several younger sisters" (Freud, 1985, pp. 230–231).

How does Freud know this? He presents no evidence that his father actually abused his siblings. Psychoanalyst Kurt Eissler views Freud's accusations against his father as containing improbabilities that make it "an unsolved conundrum" (Eissler, 2001, p. 163). Sigmund's charges against Jakob are a great unexplained leap. Still, from December 1896 to August 1897, Freud is enthralled by the paternal etiology thesis.

It was only four months after Jakob died that Freud described his father as a sexual pervert. He is no longer acting like a son feeling poignant loss. Instead, Freud's own internal dynamics take center stage. On May 31, 1897, Sigmund interprets a dream of his as indicating that he "had overaffectionate feelings for Mathilde," his eldest daughter. He then writes to Fliess that this dream fulfills his wish to catch fathers as "the originator of neurosis" and his interpretation of the meaning of the dream "puts an end to any ever-recurring doubts" (Freud, 1985, p. 249). Four months after accusing his father, on June 22, 1897, Freud tells Fliess, "I have been through some kind of neurotic experience" (Freud, 1985, p. 254). On August 14, 1897, Freud further diagnoses himself and refers to "My little hysteria" (Freud, 1985, p. 261). Thirty-eight days later, on September 21, 1897, Freud suddenly makes another leap. He tells Fliess of his "surprise that in all cases, the *father*, not excluding my own, had to be accused of being perverse" (Freud, 1985, p. 264).

Freud had written that the hysteria of his siblings was caused by Jakob's perversions. Would it not follow that Sigmund's little hysteria would also be caused by the sexual abuse of his father? The conjunction of recognizing his own being a hysteric with his contention that Sigmund's siblings problems were caused by Jakob's perversions may have been more than he could psychologically bear. When Freud's 1936 statement that criticizing the father leading to guilt is applied to him in 1897, he might have developed much internal regret for saying Jakob was a sexual pervert.

As mentioned, not even six weeks after the August 1897 declaration of his own hysteria, Sigmund begins trying to convince himself that fathers are not culpable. His writings take various psychological paths in pursuit of this effort. He was arguing with himself against what he formerly and boldly asserted.

In a letter to Fliess on September 21, 1897, Freud replaced his sexual seduction theory with one where it is not actual abuse but the child's fantasies that are the causal factors. He said that "there are no indications of reality in the unconscious," and so "one cannot distinguish between truth and fiction that has been cathected by affect." Hysterics have unconscious reasons to accuse their elders, and so "sexual fantasy invariably seizes upon the theme of the parents." He also asserts that actual "widespread perversions against children are not very probable." In 1925, Freud looks back on what he figured out in September 1897. He wrote that "as far as the neuroses was concerned psychic reality was of more importance than material reality" (Freud, 1959 [1925], SEXX, p. 34).

How can Freud be sure that the material reality of sexual abuse of children was not widespread? His assertion that in every case it is the male parent who needs to be suspected contradicts his finding from 1896 of diverse perpetrators. Freud is reversing himself and jumping to conclusions. Supporting evidence is not provided. The paternal etiology thesis for Freud psychologically became a hot potato he was quickly dropping. He is a man internally at struggle with his own claims and assertions.

Just because there is unconscious fantasy, of course, does not mean that sexual abuse is absent. On the one hand, Freud in September 1897 is claiming that the unconscious blurs the line between fantasy and reality, while, on the other hand, in the 1896 hysteria articles, Freud claimed to have obtained evidence on who the abusers actually were. It is worth looking at these earlier findings and how Freud abandoned them.

In his first of these earlier articles, he claimed to have carried "out a complete psycho-analysis in thirteen cases of hysteria." His findings then did not point primarily to fathers. Instead, Freud reports that in "seven out of the thirteen cases the intercourse was between children on both sides," usually a girl and her brother (Freud, 1962 [1896], SE III, p. 152). This would indicate that seizing on the parents may not have always been the case.

Later in 1896, he says he now had treated eighteen cases of hysteria and finds three categories of perverted abusers: assaults on female children by strangers; abuse by adults looking after the child, a nurse, governess, tutor, or close relative; or the aforementioned sexual relationship between a brother and sister. Significantly, he also reported that "in most of my cases I found two or more of these aetiologies were in operation together," for regularly "sexual experiences" for these exploited children were "coming from different quarters" (Freud, 1962 [1896], SE III, pp. 207–208). This means that there were more often at least two different perpetrators acting independently of each other. So, when in September 1897, he says it was always fathers that had to be suspected of sexually abusing children, something seems askew. In the autumn of 1897, Freud discarded his earlier research on who sexually abused children; he ignores, forgets, or contradicts his own prior empirical findings.

What we have in the September 21, 1897 letter is a complex maneuver. The declaration of the primacy of the unconscious is inseparable from downgrading the frequency of sexual abuse. It also suddenly discounts the previous accusations that fathers are the perpetrators, and acts as if the 1896 findings on hysteria did not exist. As sexual abuse of children and unconscious fantasies can co-exist, then fathers could be perpetrators. From the September 21 letter on, Sigmund Freud was reversing gears. Instead of blaming fathers, including his own, he was now actively pursuing finding ways that fathers could be absolved.

What is also striking is that despite his declaration that it was fantasy and not reality, in subsequent letters to Fliess, he sometimes ignores that conclusion. For instance, as part of his 1897 self-analysis, Freud tried to find what led him to become a hysteric. In this search, he does not focus on internal fantasies but is looking for an actual abuser.

On October 3 and 4, 1897, Freud reports "that in my case the 'prime originator' was an ugly, elderly but clever woman," his nannie. He describes her as being "my teacher in sexual matters," and gives specifics. Instead of fantasy, he has now found a culprit who acted sexually with him when he was under three years old. This allows him to declare "that the old man plays no active part in my case" (Freud, 1985, pp. 268–269). Wait a minute! Freud had previously found that in most cases there was more than one perpetrator. He now ignores that claim in a rush to exclude the possibility that his father was sexually abusive. This is an eager impulse to declare his father to be innocent. That Sigmund now acquits his father in his own case indicates that the son likely had suspected that his father may have been the originator of his hysteria.

If his father in relation to him was not a pervert, what about with his younger siblings? What is remarkable is that Freud makes no further reference to the earlier claim that his father abused his younger brother and some sisters. In the letters to Fliess, there is no further reference to Sigmund's over affectionate feelings toward Mathilde. The subject of his sibling's hysteria and sexual interest in Mathilde just disappears.

Freud, Oedipus, Laius

But his efforts to move away from fathers as perverts and abusers are not done. His next major assertion in this extraordinary journey also downplays paternal perversions. In the same month that Freud found his own hysteria was not caused by his father, he announced the Oedipus complex to Fliess. This new idea also grew out of his self-analysis. In October 1897, Sigmund asked his mother if she remembered this nurse whom he had claimed was his sexual teacher. His mother did, and this led Freud to recall that this elderly woman had been removed from his life when he was a youngster of three or so in Freiberg. Part of this memory was that Sigmund had been afraid that as his nannie was missing and that once he found that his mother too was absent, he became very upset. "I was crying in despair." He called on his adult half-brother Philipp to help, which he did. When his mother showed up "slender and beautiful," the boy was relieved.

In recounting to himself these memories, a light bulb went off in Sigmund's head. He tells Fliess, "A single idea of general interest dawned on me. I have found in my own case too [the phenomenon of] being in love with my mother and jealous of my father, and I now consider it a universal event in early childhood." Freud then proceeds to connect these feelings to Sophocles' drama, *Oedipus Rex*. "Everyone in the audience was once a budding Oedipus in fantasy" (Freud, 1985, pp. 271–272).

And so was born the idea of a universal Oedipus complex. It remained a cornerstone of psychoanalysis from its inception to Freud's death and beyond. As philosopher Patricia Kitcher concludes, "Nothing was more central or more original in psychoanalysis than the postulation of the Oedipus complex" (Kitcher, 1992, p. 107). Freud himself declared, "I venture to say that if psycho-analysis could boast of no other achievement than the discovery of the repressed Oedipus complex that alone would give it a claim to be included among the precious new acquisitions of mankind" (Freud, 1964 [1939], SE XXIII, pp. 192–193). When in 1900, Freud first publicly proclaimed this discovery, these incestuous wishes of love of mother and jealousy of father, he wrote they "have been forced upon us by Nature" (Freud, 1953 [1900], SE IV, p. 263).

The way that Freud formulated this newly discovered complex reversed his sexual seduction thesis. With the Oedipal theory, the adults and siblings were basically acquitted, and the boy's desires and jealousy were to blame. To reach his bold conclusion Freud was highly selective in what he included and omitted from the full myth of Oedipus. In "Greek myths," according to the findings of Siegfried Zepf and collaborators, "the father's brutality is the reason for the son's violence against him" (Zepf et al., 2017, p. 30). Freud was aware of this aspect of the father's role in the Oedipus myth, but gave the murderous intentions of the father toward the son little or no place in the psychological dynamics of the Oedipus complex.

Freud also omitted another crucial element in this tale. The prophecy against Laius came following Oedipus's father earlier rape of the boy Chrissipus. "Laius was deemed to have been the inventor of pederasty," writes anthropologist and psychoanalyst George Devereux (Devereux, 1988 [1953], p. 100). This made Oedipus's father a sexual pervert who committed the very sexual abuse that Freud had previously said was the cause of hysteria. Freud was likely familiar with this side of the complete Oedipus myth as he cited works by both Roscher and Constans that discuss various configurations of the Oedipus tales in Greek mythology (Zepf et al., 2017, p. 5). This likely knowledge makes curious his choice of the Oedipus myth as grounds for focusing on the child's desires while leaving out a crucial part of the father's actions.

Psychoanalyst John Munder Ross writes "it is remarkable that Freud should have ignored Laius' active part in the narrative," and adds that few later analysts "fill in the gaps. The blind spots are reminiscent of Oedipus' own assumption of the entire burden of guilt... as if exculpating the dead father altogether" (Ross, 1994, p. 98). The question of the causes of neuroses had become highly personal to Freud. As Ross says, in moving from paternal etiology to the child's dynamics Freud sought to absolve fathers from being sexual perverts. Historian Larry Wolff concurs. For Freud in "consigning the murderous wishes to childhood...Freud quietly, implicitly ruled out" that there could be such "wishes against children themselves." This "omission was not incidental....the entire formulation of the Oedipus complex... was entirely conceived as a problem of the child" (Wolff, 1988, p. 200).

These observations echo Devereux's declaration that the "Oedipus complex is rooted in the adult's deep-seated need to place all responsibility for the Oedipus complex upon the child and to ignore, whenever possible" the role of the parents in this phenomenon (Devereux, 1988 [1953], p. 98). Freud's omissions are telling. What he leaves out returns to the phenomenon of fathers as sexual abusers. This takes place in the very assertion that it is the child's feelings and wishes rather than parental perversion that leads to neurosis. The complete Oedipus myth then gives ground to affirm the perversion of fathers that Freud now seeks to disconfirm. At the same time as Freud is opening doors, he is trying to run away from something.

He has gone from one extreme to another. Earlier in 1896, there were multiple abusers identified, and parents being just one among them. Then suddenly he reverses himself and says that more and more fathers are the abusers. Even later, he declares that in all cases it had to be the father. Then another alteration, it is not abuse but unconscious fantasy that causes hysteria. Later, it cannot be fathers that are central to aggressive feelings, but the sexual desire of the son for his mother. The aggression and sexual abuse of a father are completely omitted. With the Oedipus complex Freud has succeeded in his efforts to downplay fathers who previously were the main cause of abuse and aggression. Freud has quickly journeyed from indicting to acquitting fathers as sexual abusers. The absolving is accompanied by downplaying real psychologically threatening events. The psychoanalytic Rubicon has been crossed.

Freudian psychoanalysis was often, if not always, built on the unconscious over the actual, rather than a synthesis of the real and the imaginary. Keeping the distance between the two enabled dismissing his own charges against fathers. Freud's journey in September and October 1897 goes from denying fathers were regularly abusers to the Oedipus complex, which switches focus from fathers to sons. This seems to have done wonders for Sigmund's psychological well-being and theoretical innovations. Yet it may work better for Freud's frame of mind than it does as a balanced theory.

Sigmund Freud could have developed a theory that integrated the desires of the child and the intent and actions of the father, yet alone the mother. But he did not. He did not choose in 1897 to connect the centrality of parental fantasies with childhood fantasies, how they intersect, and the dynamics that result. A central focus of his thought in late 1897 was to move attention away from fathers and toward sons, and so he omits much that is pertinent. His path from the 1896 articles on hysteria to the next year's declaration of the Oedipus complex are filled with puzzlements and quandaries. As innovative as Freud's assertions are, each step following the 1896 hysteria papers is filled with little evidence, a rush to judgment, and an eagerness to be free of something that troubles Freud's uneasy conscience.

The Oedipal theories grew out of Freud's personal experience. Writing about Sigmund's initial Oedipal formulation, psychologist Robert Holt says, "it seems audacious to the point of foolhardiness to jump from self-observation to a general law" (Holt, 1989, p. 53). As Freud's former mentor, Josef Breuer, in 1907 said, "Freud is a man given to absolute and exclusive formulations...which, in my opinion, leads to excessive generalizations" (in Holt, 1989, pp. 50–51). Psychologist Frank Tallis: Freud "seems to have projected his own Oedipal preoccupations on the entire human race, past and present" (Tallis, 2024, p. 183). Freud's great leaps, of course, led to innovative notions that have altered the conceptions of many of what it is to be human. His version of the Oedipus myth served its psychological function of discarding the paternal etiology thesis.

Clearly, Freud's rush to judgment about fathers as sexual abusers, his later absolving fathers, and the universality of love of mother and jealousy of father are not disinterested observations. They are all connected to the very personal nature of Freud's struggles following Jakob's 1896 death. Sigmund Freud's emerging doctrines were inseparable from his own preoccupation with the sins of the fathers and his own self-described neurosis and hysteria. We cannot understand the ways Freud structured his ideas separate from his internal divisions. With the discovery of the unconscious, the abandonment of the "seduction theory," and the proclamation of the Oedipus complex, the internal dynamics of Freud's psyche and his doctrines are all interconnected. His great discoveries are part and parcel of his internal dynamics.

The Internal and External

As noted, another aspect of Freud's psychological divisions is his moving from abuse committed by adults and siblings to the Oedipus complex. Freud is now shying away from integrating the internal and external, fantasy and reality. Here the Freudian internal refers to the thoughts, wishes, and desires of the child, plus the internal images he or she has toward other persons and objects. The external is material reality in the variety of its familial, cultural, historical, intellectual, and religious forms.

His challenges with the relationship of the internal and external are noticed by others. Peter Gay in discussing the famous September 21, 1897, letter admits that if "the ground of reality had been lost, that of fantasy had been won" (Gay, 1989, p. 96). Physician and psychoanalyst Willard Gaylin finds that Freud "tended to ignore the environment in which the isolated self would be nurtured or deprived" (Gaylin, 1990, p. 114). Philosopher and psychoanalyst Joel Whitebook wrote that "Freud's position in 1900…suffered from a degree of perhaps unavoidable one-sidedness" (Whitebook, 2017, p. 223). Psychoanalyst Abram Kardiner finds that Freudians are convinced "that they do not need to concern themselves with the cultural environment," which to Kardiner "must be taken into account" though Freud and his followers have "no technique for so doing" (Kardiner, 1959, p. 85). Hans Loewald writes that Freud views "external reality…in the aspect of a hostile, threatening power" for the ego (Loewald, 1980 [1951], pp. 3–4). Nancy Chodorow writes, "The 'real external world,' that is, the social and the cultural, and the links between psychoanalysis and the social, have gone missing…in our theories, our interests, and our interdisciplinary curiosity" (Chodorow, 2020, p. 59).

As the impact of the external can be downplayed, the fear of the father's actions and the guilt over making such severe accusations against Jakob can be attempted to be swept under the psychological rug. We have in the twists and turns of his

1897 letters the great Freudian paradox: he combines self-reversal with his revelations about the unconscious that show exceptional insight. In addition, his one-sidedness in not more fully interconnecting the internal and the external makes his findings a partial portrait of the unconscious.

Another sign of Freud's uneasy incompleteness is that at times, he distorts his own findings. For instance, in 1933, recalling the period when he saw hysteria as caused by a variety of sexual abusers, Freud says that "almost all my women patients told me that they had been seduced by their father" (Freud, 1964 [1933], SE XXII, p. 120). Kurt Eissler corrects Freud's statement, "Nowhere in his publications of that period does one encounter women accusing their fathers." This, Eissler says, applies to both the *Studies on Hysteria* and to the 1896 published papers on hysteria (Eissler, 2001, p. 216). What Freud's 1933 misrepresentation of his own writings enables him to do is to claim that "these reports were untrue" and were "derived from phantasies and not from real occurrences" (Freud, 1964 [1933], SE XXII, p. 120). This claim does not fit with his 1896 reports that it was siblings more than fathers who the charges were leveled against by the victims.

In Freud's effort to absolve fathers, including within his own family, the die is cast. During the rest of his career, from time to time, he goes back and forth, but more often than not he underplays the full connection of the real and the imagined.

The bulk of part two of this book will present examples of where Freud's inner psychological divisions are reflected in the one-sidedness of his doctrines. Now I wish to present examples from Freud that has stark similarities to his downgrading the frequency of sexual abuse of children. It is another instance where traumatic events can impact someone's well-being, and where Freud finds a way of discounting the external reality. The first instance involves a couple of lesser-known articles on the soldier's psychological traumas during the First World War.

Freud and the External: War Trauma

Freud examined what at the time was called shell shock during and after the 1914–1918 Great War. The horrors of trench warfare, with their astounding casualty rates transformed Western culture's perspective on itself. In addition to the millions of fatalities was the psychological toll of the deadly violence for the combatants. In two lesser-known writings from 1919 and 1920, Freud addresses the traumas of soldiers.

In 1919, he says that the neurosis of war has been "made possible" by "a conflict in the ego" (Freud, 1955 [1919], SE XVII, p. 209). The next year, he says "the immediate cause of all war neurosis was an unconscious inclination…to withdraw from…active service. Fear of losing his life, opposition to the command to kill other people" and rebellion against military obedience "were the most important affective sources." Experiencing the actual terrors of combat is not included in this litany. Freud then adds: "with the end of the war the war neurotics too, disappeared." This to Freud is "impressive proof of the psychical causation of their illnesses" (Freud, 1955 [1920], SE XVIII, pp. 212–213, 215). How does he know trauma faded away? As with Freud's 1897 claim that widespread sexual abuse of children is not very probable, his conclusion that traumatic responses disappeared after the war is striking. It does fit his theories, yet he provides no documentation to back up his assertion. In both instances, Freud's statements reinforce his predilection for internal causes more than an interconnection between actual reality and internal dynamics. It is unfortunate that Freud chose to downplay traumatic experiences of being a child sexually abused and being in combat for lengthy periods.

After all, there is ample evidence that "war neuroses" did not fade away after the 1918 armistice was signed. As Benjamin Butterworth reports, the psychological trauma of combat in the First World War

> had an unprecedented toll on veterans, many of whom suffered symptoms for the rest of their lives. These ranged from distressing memories that veterans found difficult to forget, to extreme episodes of catatonia and terror when reminded of their trauma.
>
> (Butterworth, 2018)

Post-war, a number of veterans were treated for the lingering impact of their war trauma. One psychiatrist who worked with such troubled veterans in the Brooklyn Veteran's Hospital in the 1920s was Abram Kardiner, who had been analyzed by Freud. These individuals were still showing symptoms years after the First World War ended (Kardiner, 1941).

Again, Freud characteristically underemphasized the external as a central cause of trauma. He was not often interested in exploring how the dreadful reality of war, or for that matter being sexually abused as a child, could alter one's internal being and produce long-lasting traumatic reactions. In other words, psychic realities can be shaped by external traumas. His war essays reflect his being more focused on the internal than the interconnections between psychic and material realities.

In his discounting the frequency of sexual abuse and his claim that war trauma disappeared when the war ended are just two important examples of how Freud turned to opinion more than evidence. Freud was often better at developing ideas than in searching for ways to empirically confirm them.

Freud and the External: Childhood Sexual Abuse

Freud's downplaying the persistence of war trauma re-opens the questions of both the frequency and long-term impact of children who have been sexually abused. This abuse as a youngster is just one component of adverse childhood experiences. These childhood traumas have recently become more empirically studied.

Here is where this research originated. A large U.S. HMO in the 1990s mailed 13,494 questionnaires to adults about adverse childhood experiences, about 70% responded. Individuals who had four or more such adverse experience had a four to twelvefold increase risks for alcoholism, drug abuse, depression, and suicide attempts. They also had a graded relationship to having ischemic heart disease, cancer, chronic lung disease, skeletal fractures, and liver disease (Felitti, et al., 1998). Five of the top ten leading causes of death are associated with adverse childhood experiences, and one in six adults surveyed experienced four or more types of adverse childhood experiences (Center for Disease Control, 2020).

As childhood sexual abuse is one of these adverse childhood experiences, three Texas A&M researchers singled it out to empirically study. They conducted a survey of non-institutionalized adults on the topic and received 10,624 responses. This was a survey. It did not include medical findings reported by physicians, as was done in the earlier study described above. Overall, for males and females, 10.26% as children had either been touched sexually by someone at least five years older than them, had been directed to touch someone sexually over five years older than them, or had forced sexual intercourse. For girls, the total was 14.66% and for boys 5.60%. While Freud in 1897 without conducting any research declared sexual abuse of children was not frequent, it turns out in at least one large sample it was. Noticeably, girls were much more sexually abused than boys. There were also long-term mental health consequences. Compared to those not abused, those abused as children were much more likely to report 14 or more days per month of being mentally unhealthy and of having poor physical health (Downing et al., 2021).

Oddly enough issues of parental abuse of children made headlines in Vienna at the end of 1899. The first instance in October 1899 was of an unmarried mother killing her daughter and self in the woods outside Vienna. The next month a trial was held about a mother and father who had tortured their five-year-old daughter until she died. A few weeks later another case led to sensational headlines. A father and stepmother had killed one of their offspring and mutilated seven other children. Child abuse had led to sensational accounts becoming news stories in the Vienna papers (Wolff, 1998, pp. 3–4). According to historian Larry Wolff, "Freud avoided the cases altogether." By that time, for the father of psychoanalysis, Wolff says, "child abuse was, in fact deeply problematic." Freud had "consigned the murderous wish to childhood....Freud quietly, implicitly, ruled out consideration" that parents could have lethal "wishes against children themselves" (Wolff, 1998, pp. 199–200). At the end of 1899, he did not appear to be receptive to include parental torture and murdering their own children in his reflections. As such, he clearly minimized how parental violence toward their own offspring could become an integral part of psychoanalytic doctrine. The impact on a child's psychic reality of being abused and tortured, of experiencing intense adverse childhood experiences, let alone their consequences, was by and large omitted from Freudian psychoanalysis after 1897. External reality was not as important to Freud as documenting the internal psychic world.

What is important is that like war trauma, sexually abused children suffer over a long term. Freud without evidence sought to downplay the frequency and the long-term consequences of war trauma and sexual abuse. The suffering endured by both groups was not something that after 1897 that Freud consistently brought front and center. He was more concerned with children's sexual desires than their being sexually abused by older perpetrators. Nor did Freud after late 1897 center in on how much more frequent sexual abuse of girls than boys are. From late 1897 forward, Freud's lack of recognition, concern, or empathy for the long-term sufferings from war trauma and those sexually abused are noticeable and revealing.

Conclusion

Sigmund Freud's work is in some ways a great paradox. Hardly anyone else in the history of Western thought has been so willing to plunge the depths of the human heart. Yet he also made decisions that created significant blind spots and omissions. He also denied and distorted his own intellectual history as a way to not face what he wishes to evade about himself and his doctrines.

Many of us need to recognize how those views we now oppose may have some lingering hold on us. From Socrates onward, a number of thinkers have proclaimed that self-knowledge is our goal. Self-deception may be our demon. Even Freud, who went to the depths, evaded some of his own psychological dilemmas and divisions. The Freud of the 1890s and afterwards both developed psychoanalysis into an invaluable enterprise, and regularly sought to deny what he had earlier affirmed. His divided internal dialectic was fully present in his life and thought.

It is not unusual in human endeavors for great discoveries to contain denials, gaps, and blind spots. Freud evolved into one of the boldest, most innovative, and fertile thinkers Western culture has ever seen. At the same time, he retained an internal dialectic, an argument within himself that left his doctrines one sided and incomplete. He did not consistently seek to interconnect the unconscious with external phenomenon, which leaves huge holes in his conception of unconscious psychic reality. Like many of us, Freud was a mixture of opposites. We do him justice as a fellow human in recognizing his personal and intellectual struggles and evasions along with his genius.

There are few of us who can avoid having our divisions' impact on our ideas. Fewer still who are as innovative and fertile as Sigmund Freud was. As we should learn from his and our own limitations, so can we continue the search for humanity's inner core, our self-inflicted horrors, and astounding creative wonders.

The approach in this work is to document how Freud's personal internal divisions are important in understanding his doctrinal problems and the sufficiency of his favoring the psychic over the material without seeking to interconnect them. I adhere to what some others maintain. As noted earlier, I am in accord with Peter Rudnytsky's statement that "the achievements of creative thinkers and writers have their roots in the soil of personal experience." And with James Anderson's contention that in studying a "psychoanalysts...life and work, we especially want to see the relevance of their personal experience to their chief concepts." Sigmund Freud as a thinker cannot be understood separate from the ways his struggles over his father shaped his development of psychoanalysis from 1897 to his death.

References

Breger, L. (2000). *Freud: Darkness in the midst of vision.* John Wiley & Sons.

Butterworth, B. (2018). What World War I taught us About PTSD. *The Conversation.* https://theconversation.com/what-world-war-i-taught-us-about-ptsd-105613/

Center for Disease Control (2020). Adverse childhood experience in U.S. adults, https://search.yahoo.com/search;_ylt=AwrEpUePStto_AEAEghXNyoA;_ylu=Y29sbwNiZjEEcG9z AzEEdnRpZAMEc2VjA3JlbC1ib3Q-?type=E210US1494G0&p=center+for+disease+control+adverse+childhood+2020+pdf&fr2=p%3As%2Cv%3Aw%2Cm%3Ars-bottom%2Cct%3Agossip&fr=mcafee.

Chodorow, N. (2020). *The psychoanalytic ear and the sociological eye.* Routledge.

Clark, R. (1980). *Freud: The man and the cause.* Random House.

Devereux, G. (1988). Why Oedipus killed Laius: A note on the complementary Oedipus complex in Greek drama. *The Oedipus papers* (G. Pollock and J. M. Ross Eds). International Universities Press, pp. 97–116 (Original work published 1953).

Downing, N. et al. (2021). The impact of childhood sexual abuse and adverse childhood experiences on adult health related quality of life. *Child Abuse and Neglect.* Volume 120, October 2021, 105181.

Eissler, K. R. (2001). *Freud and the seduction theory: A brief love affair.* International Universities Press.

Freud, S. (1953). *The standard edition of the complete psychological works of Sigmund Freud, Volume IV.* (J. Strachey Ed. and Trans.). The Hogarth Press (Original work published 1900).

Freud, S. (1955). *Totem and taboo, The standard edition of the complete psychological works of Sigmund Freud, Volume XIII* (J. Strachey Ed. and Trans.). The Hogarth Press, pp. 1–162 (Original work published 1913).

Freud, S. (1955). Introduction to *Psycho-analysis and the war neuroses, The standard edition of the complete psychological works of Sigmund Freud, Volume XVII* (J. Strachey Ed. and Trans.). The Hogarth Press, pp. 205–210 (Original work published 1919).

Freud. S. (1955). Memorandum on the electrical treatment of war neurotics. *The standard edition of the complete psychological works of Sigmund Freud, Volume XVIII* (J. Strachey Ed. and Trans.). The Hogarth Press, pp. 210–215 (Original work published 1920).

Freud, S. (1959). An autobiographical study, *The standard edition of the complete psychological works of Sigmund Freud Volume XX* (j. Strachey Ed. and Trans.). The Hogarth Press, pp. 1-71 (original work published 1925).

Freud, S (1960). *The standard edition of the complete psychological works of Sigmund Freud, Volume VI* (J. Strachey Ed. and Trans.). The Hogarth Press (Original work published 1901).

Freud, S. (1960). *Letters of Sigmund Freud* (E. Freud Ed., T. and J. Stern, Trans.). Basic Books.

Freud, S. (1962). *The standard edition of the complete psychological works of Sigmund Freud, Volume III* (J. Strachey Ed. and Trans.). The Hogarth Press (Original work published 1896).

Freud, S. (1964). *New introductory lectures on psycho-analysis. The standard edition of the complete psychological works of Sigmund Freud, Volume XXII* (J. Strachey Ed. and Trans.). The Hogarth Press, pp. 5–182 (Original work published 1933).

Freud, S. (1964). A disturbance of memory on the acropolis. *The standard edition of the complete psychological works of Sigmund Freud, Volume XXII* (J. Strachey Ed. and Trans.). The Hogarth Press, pp. 239–248 (Original work published 1936).

Freud, S. (1964). *An outline of psycho-analysis. The standard edition of the complete psychological works of Sigmund Freud, Volume XXIII* (J. Strachey Ed. and Trans.). The Hogarth Press, pp. 192–193 (Original work published 1939).

Freud, S. (1985). *The complete letters of Sigmund Freud to Wilhelm Fliess 1887–1904.* (J. M. Masson Ed. and Trans.). Harvard University Press.

Gay, P. (1989), *Freud: A life for our time.* W. W. Norton & Company.

Gaylin, W. (1990). *On being and becoming human.* Penguin Books.

Holt, R. (1989). *Freud reappraised: A fresh look at psychoanalytic theory.* The Guilford Press.

Kardiner, A. (1959). Cultural Implications of Psychoanalysis. *Psychoanalysis, scientific method, and philosophy* (S. Hook, Ed.) pp. 81–103. New York University Press.

Kitcher, P. (1992). *Freud's dream: A complete interdisciplinary science of mind.* The MIT Press.

Loewald, H. (1980). *Papers on psychoanalysis.* Yale University Press.

Montaigne, M. (1943). *The complete works* (D. Frame, Trans.). Everyman's Library.

Ross, J. M. (1994). *What men want: Mothers, fathers and manhood.* Harvard University Press.

Tallis, F. (2024). *Mortal secrets: Freud, Vienna, and the discovery of the modern mind.* St. Martin's Press.

Whitebook, J. (2017). *Freud: An intellectual biography.* Cambridge University Press.

Wolff, L. (1988). *Child abuse in Freud's Vienna.* New York University Press.

Zepf, S. (2017). Civilization and its discontents – A reappraisal. *Asian Social Science,* Volume 13, No. 4, pp. 93–103.

Chapter 2

Fathers and Sons

Freud's Discovery of the Oedipus Complex

I now approach Freud's Oedipal discoveries from a different angle. It is one that illustrates the mixture of the internal and external. Freud's Oedipal theory centers on the nuclear family of mother, father, and child. Yet when Freud recounts his coming upon the Oedipus complex, it concerns a time he was residing in a close extended family. Later, when Freud himself revisits this period of time, it turns out that there can be more than three players in Oedipal dynamics. Reviewing the early years of Sigmund Freud's existence in conjunction with the Oedipus complex illustrates that the official Freudian conception of the Oedipal triad is at odds with his interpretation of his personal experience.

Of course, the Oedipus complex is central to Freudian psychoanalysis. "I venture to say that if psycho-analysis could boast of no other achievement than the discovery of the repressed Oedipus complex," Freud writes in his last book, "that alone would give it a claim to be included among the precious new acquisitions of mankind" (Freud, 1964 [1940], *SE XXIII*, pp. 192–193). Philosopher Patricia Kitcher (1992) says: "Nothing was more central or more original in psycho analysis than the postulation of the Oedipus complex and its 'heir', the superego" (p. 107).

Freud proclaims that "the Oedipus complex... has become the shibboleth that distinguishes the adherents of psycho-analysis from its opponents" (Freud, 1953 [1905], *SE VII*, p. 226). He believes that "the beginnings of religion, morals, society and art converge in the Oedipus complex" (Freud, 1955 [1913], *SE XIII*, p. 156). Not only did civilization for him originate with the Oedipus complex; it was also a universal phenomenon. "Every new arrival on this planet," Freud declares, "is faced by the task of mastering the Oedipus complex" (Freud, 1953 [1905], *SE VII*, p. 226). It is not surprising then that Freud considers the Oedipus complex to be one of the major cornerstones of psychoanalytic theory, along with the unconscious, repression, resistance, and sexuality (Freud, 1955 [1923], *SE XVIII*, p. 247).

The paths by which Freud comes to the Oedipus complex are multiple. It is a tale by itself, with its own internal drama and subtexts. This story reveals the inner tensions and denials at the very heart of this cornerstone of psychoanalytic theory. We have described one of the paths by which Freud discovered the Oedipus complex. Here is another. For Freud's journey to this central phenomenon combines a search for the causes of hysteria with his self-analysis. This paper will show how

DOI: 10.4324/9781041074717-4

Freud's discovery of the nuclear complex is also connected with the dynamics of his early family life. In Freud's initial conception of the Oedipus complex, there are ambiguities and confusions. While the previous chapter demonstrated Freud's internal drama, this chapter focuses more on the external. It includes not only Jakob and Sigismund, but other family members and places the Oedipal triad within the family romance.

Throughout his psychoanalytic career, Freud vacillates over what causes neurosis. From time to time, Freud would recognize that his theories had not pinpointed the origins of mental illness. In 1926, he ·wrote, "we have once more come…upon the riddle which has so often confronted us: whence does neurosis come?…After tens of years of psychoanalytic labors, we are as much in the dark about this problem as we were at the start" (Freud, 1959 [1926], *SE XX*, pp. 148–149).

This darkness stems from Freud's divided allegiances, intellectually and personally. To comprehend these divisions and how they affect the fate of the Oedipus complex, a double line of exposition will be pursued: the personal and familial roots of Freud's preoccupations will be entwined with his theoretical investigations. The Oedipus complex cannot be fully understood without seeing its roots in Freud's view of his own childhood and family life. We have to return to the external in Freud's life to understand his internal paths to the Oedipal doctrine.

Freud's Family Romance

Sigismund Freud was born on 6 May 1856 in Freiberg, Moravia, a town of 5,000 in Austria. He himself shortened his first name to Sigmund. His father, Jakob Freud, a wool merchant, was born in 1815. Amalie Nathanson Freud, his mother, was 20 years younger than her husband. This, however, was only the beginning of the complication in Freud's family constellation. Jakob had been married before. His first wife, Sally Kanner, bore him two sons: Emmanuel and Philipp. These two brothers were nearly the same age as their stepmother, Amalie. At the time of Sigismund's birth, both his elder half-brothers lived in Freiberg. Philipp was unmarried and resided across the street from his father. Emmanuel also lived nearby with his wife, Maria, and their son John who was born on 1 August 1855. On 20 November 1856, Maria gave birth to a daughter, Pauline. Young Sigismund was uncle to his older nephew, John, and was just six months older than his niece, Pauline. Emmanuel's family was so intimate with Jakob's that, according to Ernest Jones, "the two families might be regarded as almost one" (Jones, 1953, p. 6). It is not clear what happened to Jakob's first wife, Sally Kanner Freud. In the 1852 register of Jews resident in Freiberg, and in the passport register of 31 October 1852, Sally is not listed as Jakob's wife. Instead, one Rebecca Freud, a woman in her early thirties, is entered as the spouse of the same Jakob Freud. Yet, the July 1855 marriage certificate of Sigismund's parents stated that Jakob had been a widower since 1852 (Krull, 1986, p. 267).

Was it Sally or Rebecca who expired in 1852? Who was Rebecca and what happened to her? She makes this sudden appearance in the Freiberg records in 1852, but is not present in the 1854 town records. Neither Sigismund nor any of his relatives ever mentioned Rebecca or that Jakob had three wives. Even without these puzzles about the existence of Rebecca and the fate of Sally, Sigismund's family relations were significantly complex.

There was, after all, a strange mixture of the generations in the Freiberg Freud family. Ronald Clark writes: "Sigismund's 20-year old mother was as young as, or younger than, her stepsons. His father was old enough to be his grandfather, his mother young enough to be his sister" (Clark, 1980, p. 4). Also present in the house was a nannie, an older woman. Ernest Jones says,

> It "was not unnatural" that the young Sigismund "should pair off Jakob and Nannie, the two forbidding authorities. Then came Emmanuel with his wife, and there remained Philipp and Amalie who were just of an age. All this appeared very tidy and logical, but still there was the awkward fact that Jakob, not Philipp, slept in the same bed as Amalie. It was all very puzzling."
>
> (Jones, 1953, p. 11)

Also unusual was that nephew John and niece Pauline probably called Jakob grandfather, while Sigismund would address him as father.

Didier Anzieu contends that "the riddle of kinship" was the "prime motivation for' Freud's 'scientific curiosity" (Anzieu, 1986, p. 247). "The course of Freud's emotional evolution," Peter Gay writes, "was shaped by the bewildering texture of familial relationships he found very hard to sort out" (Gay, 1988, p. 5). Freud's "restless search into the meaning of humanity and human relations," Jones declares, was "first generated in connection with the puzzling problems of his early family life" (Jones, 1953, p. 33).

There were other unsettling family occurrences in Freud's early years. A brother to Sigismund, Julius, was born in October 1857, but died in April 1858. Freud writes that he "greeted" this brother "with adverse wishes and genuine childhood jealousy; and that his death left the germ of (self-) reproaches in me" (Freud, 1985, p. 268). Eight months after Julius's death, Amalie gave birth to a daughter, Anna, in December 1858. Sigismund writes that he "was very far from approving of this addition to the family" (Freud, 1960 [1901], *SE VI*, p. 51). In addition, on 22 February 1859, Sigismund became an uncle again; a daughter, Bertha, was born to Emmanuel and Maria.

In the summer of that same year, 1859, all the Freuds departed from Freiberg, Philipp along with Emmanuel and his family eventually settled in Manchester, England; while Jakob, Amalie, and their two surviving children ended up residing in Vienna. The Jakob Freud's were part of the great migration of Jews from the further reaches of the empire to the capital city. In 1857, Jews made up 1.3% of the population of Vienna. A dozen years later, they were 6.6% of the city's residents (Oxaal and Weitzmann, 1985, p. 398). When Jews were granted civil rights in the 1840s and equality under the law in 1867, they seized these opportunities and became urbanized.

The city-dwelling Vienna Freuds became a conventional nuclear family rather than the cross-generational extended family of Freiberg. These changes may not have sat well with young Sigismund. Freud writes of the move to Vienna, "Long and difficult years followed, of which... nothing was worth remembering" (Freud, 1962 [1899], *SE* 3, p. 312). If in Freiberg he had been jealous of Julius and disapproving of Anna's arrival, he may not have welcomed the five additional siblings who appeared between 1860 and 1866. Rosa was born on 21 March 1860, Maria on 22 March 1861, Adolfine on 23 July 1862, Pauline on 3 May 1864, and Alexander on 19 April 1866. Freud's beloved mother was pregnant, nursing, or caring for infants and small children for most of Freud's formative years.

Amalie called her eldest son, "my golden Sigi." But the birth of so many siblings in such rapid succession may have reinforced Freud's dual sense of being both chosen and dethroned. Years later, he wrote that "childhood love is boundless; it demands exclusive possession, it is not content with less than all" (Freud, 1961 [1931], *SE XXI*, p. 231).

The desire for exclusive possession is connected in the boy's case, according to Freudian theory, to the mother. But this

> tie of affection, which binds the child as a rule to the parent of the opposite sex, succumbs to disappointment, to...jealousy over the birth of a new baby - unmistakable proof of the infidelity of the object of the child's affection....The lessening amount of affection he receives, the increasing demands of education, hard words and an occasional punishment - these show how at last the full extent to which he has been scorned.
>
> (Freud, 1955 [1920], *SE* XVIII, p. 21)

The consequences of this sense of being rejected are severe. "Loss of love" leaves behind "a permanent injury to self-regard in the form of a narcissistic scar" (Freud, 1955 [1920], *SE* XVIII, p. 20).

In Sigmund's case, the wound to self-esteem alternates with his sense of being his mother's favorite. His sister, Anna, just three years Freud's junior, wrote: "My mother hoped great things of her first born and treasured early incidents which gave birth to her hopes" (Bernays, 1940, p. 335). In 1933, Freud himself declared: "A mother can transfer to her son the ambition which she has been obliged to suppress in herself" (Freud, 1964 [1933], *SE* XXII, p. 133). For, as has often been noted, Freud believed that a "mother is only brought unlimited satisfaction by her relation to a son, this is altogether the most perfect, the most free from ambivalence of all human relationships" (Freud, 1964 [1933], *SE XXII*, p. 133). In this dyad, the son is not as fulfilled as the mother, even if he retains a sense of being chosen. In part, because, if the boy has a father and/or siblings, it is not only a dyad. The eldest son is pulled in opposite directions, while the mother may find more unlimited pleasure with her young son than with her husband. The seeds of the Oedipal triangle and the family complex are, to some degree, in the mother's attachment to her son.

To further complicate Sigmund's psychological development, he was not only his mother's favorite, but the whole family treated him as someone special. "Sigmund's word and wish were respected by everyone in the family," according to his sister, Anna (Bernays, 1940, p. 337). She recalls that it was nine-year-old Sigmund who selected the name Alexander for his younger brother and how at age 11 he demanded that the piano Anna and her sisters played be removed from the apartment as the sound disturbed his ability to study. She says that her brother "appealed lo my mother to remove the piano if she did not wish him to leave the house altogether" (Bernays, 1940, p. 337). It is astonishing that an 11-year-old boy in 19th-century Vienna could make such a demand of a parent and even more remarkable that it was honored. The wish of the pre-adolescent boy took precedence over the preferences of other family members. In addition, in the Freuds' apartment, Sigmund had his own room. As his son, Martin remembers this was "a privilege he alone enjoyed in the family" (Freud, 1958, p. 19).

As the exalted eldest, Sigmund acted as an authority with his siblings. He was simultaneously imperious, directive, and helpful with his sisters. He would assist them with their homework, instruct them on current events, and select their reading material. Anna said, "He exercised definite control over my reading. If I had a book that seemed to him improper for a girl of my age, he would say. 'Anna, it is too early to read that book now'" (Bernays, 1940, p. 337). His sister, Paula, told her nephew, Martin, that Sigmund would be critical to his sisters if he found them erring. He caught Paula herself spending money in a sweet shop' and 'admonished' her with 'much severity' (Freud, 1958, p. 20). Sigmund willingly assumed the role of privileged oldest sibling, even impinging sometimes on the paternal role. Martin Freud: "My father would seem to have assumed some of that responsibility even when he was young" (Freud, 1958, p. 20). Freud, a parentified child, had many reasons to confuse the roles of brother and father, to feel both privileged and rejected. Sigmund's confusion of roles between parent and child was exacerbated by the ups and downs of the Freuds in Vienna, and the role of Jakob as family provider.

Between 1860 and 1875, the family lived in six different residences. 'Poor Jews with few possessions,' historian Hannah Decker writes, 'moved often from one apartment to another' (Decker, 1991, p. 24). In their last apartment, the Freuds showed some signs of prosperity, in that they had two living rooms and three bedrooms, even though there were nine people living in this abode (Clark, 1980, p. 16). Bruno Bettelheim, a native of Vienna, declared: "Freud's parents…belonged to the Jewish middle class. For a Jewish family of the 1880s to have lived in a flat of six rooms meant that they were quite well off" (Bettelheim, 1990, p. 46). Freud himself did not perceive this affluence. In his autobiography, he wrote, "we lived in very humble circumstances" (Freud, 1959 [1925], *SE XX*, p. 8). He also spoke of "my father's generous improvidence" and "my bad financial position" (Freud, 1959 [1925], SE XX, p. 10).

How the Vienna Freuds supported themselves is something of a minor mystery. In Freiberg, Jakob had been a wool merchant, but in Vienna he was listed in neither the Vienna Trade Register nor the Trade Tax Register. Ronald Clark writes, "This apparently rules out not only his existence as a wool merchant but as any sort of trader" (Clark, 1980, p. 15). Marianne Krull states, Jacob "had no taxable income" (Krull, 1986, p. 149). There is speculation that he was a broker for out-of-town Jewish merchants and that he received assistance from his two sons in England and his wife's family. Jacob's daughter, Anna, remembers her father having "business interests" with Emmanuel and Philipp (Bernays, 1940, p. 336).

Sigmund came to view his father as ineffective financially and as the source of his own economic struggles as a young man. In 1884, he wrote to his fiancée about his father's foolish monetary schemes and the need to get assistance from Emmanuel and Philipp (Freud, 1960, p. 86). Worry over money affected not only Sigmund, but also his mother. Amalie, according to her granddaughter, Judith Bernays Heller, was "usually troubled and anxious – probably with financial worries" (Heller, 1956, p. 419). According to Sigmund's daughter, Anna, Jakob was a "rather passive man" (Young–Bruehl, 1988, p. 431). With an older, ineffective, unassertive father and a doting mother, young Sigismund took on some of the responsibilities with his sisters that were usually reserved for the parents, and became uncertain, to some extent, as to where the line between son and father was drawn. He was the chosen son with the narcissistic scar.

No matter how much or how little money they had, Jakob and Amalie resolved, according to Martin Freud, that "no sacrifice was too great" for Sigmund (Freud, 1958, p. 19). The Freuds found a way to pay for Sigmund's attendance from the age of 9 at the Sperl Gymnasium. Prior to that Jakob had tutored him at home. Sigmund excelled in school, he was the top student for seven years and was admitted to the University of Vienna at the age of 17. As Freud moved out of the Jewish environment into the secular setting, his world both expanded and became divided. The Vienna Freuds were of a generation betwixt and between the religious and educational traditions of the Jewish ghetto, with its emphasis on the study of religious texts, and the educational and professional opportunities in newly liberal Austria. On the one hand, Jakob had taught Sigmund the Old Testament, not in the original Hebrew but in the German translation of the Philippson Bible. Freud himself said: "My deep engrossment in the Bible story (almost as soon as I had learnt the art of reading) had... an enduring effect upon the direction of my interest" (Freud, 1959 [1925], *SE XX*, p. 8).

On the other hand, the Gymnasium, according to Steven Beller, taught Latin and Greek (Beller, 1989, p. 49). As an adolescent Freud was familiar with Sophocles, Shakespeare, and Goethe. He transferred the scholarly tradition of bookish Jews to the humanistic and scientific traditions of Western Europe. Historian Robert Wistrich maintains there was "a whole generation of socially and spiritually uprooted young Viennese Jews" who were "forced to live between two worlds and two cultures" (Wistrich, 1990, p. 541). Adding to Freud's inner divisions between being entitled and scorned were the external divisions of being a Jew moving in a Gentile world.

It is not surprising then that, when the time came to choose a profession, Freud felt some uncertainty. He wrote, "My initial goal" was "philosophy...when it was not yet at all clear to me to what end I was in the world" (Freud, 1985, p. 159). Despite his upbringing, Freud was trying to leave the old Jewish ways behind. He identified with what he studied at school, more than with what he had learned at home. The influence of Darwin's theories and hearing a lecture on an essay mistakenly attributed to Goethe led Freud to become a medical student (Freud, 1959 [1925], *SE XX*, p. 8). "Neither at that time, nor indeed in my later life," Freud writes, "did I feel any particular predilection for the career of a doctor. I was moved by a sort of curiosity which was...directed more towards human concerns than towards natural objects" (Freud, 1959 [1925], *SE XX*, p. 8). He "felt an overpowering need to understand something of the riddles of the world in which we live and...to contribute something to their solution" (Freud, 1959 [1926], *SE XX*, p. 253). Torn between two cultures, perplexed by an unusual family constellation, and feeling both entitled and rejected, it is not surprising that this chosen son was uncertain as to his place in the world and preoccupied by the world's mysteries. He went through a period of exploration, trying different career roles, until he found his way back to the human concerns and family issues that perplexed him.

The two structures of Freud's family constellations both seeped into his psyche. He had lived his formative years in an extended family and later in a nuclear family. Both structures seem present when Freud comes to review his Freiberg family life when coming upon Oedipal dynamics. Yet his Oedipal theory resembled more his Vienna family than the earlier one. We also see the paths within his family and in historical developments that opened up career paths for a Jew that were not present earlier in Austria's capitol city. All these occurrences and developments enabled Freud to become a physician and medical researcher. These accomplishments set the stage for his career change in his thirties. Who knows if Sigmund Freud would have been able to find his path to psychoanalysis without all these familial and professional experiences and opportunities?

After years of various scientific research and medical experiences, Freud's professional identity became consolidated when around the age of 30 he became interested in the study of hysteria. Over the next decade, there were a series of twists and turns in Freud's theories of the causes of hysteria. Then in 1896, he proposed that hysteria was brought on in adolescence or later following sexual seduction in childhood. At first, Freud said it was siblings, nurses, or close family relatives who sexually abused the child, but later he suspected that fathers, including his own, were often the ones who molested the young victims. But he became dissatisfied with these conclusions; as previously noted, on 21 September 1897 he wrote in a letter that he no longer believed in the sexual seduction theory. Freud then began combining his search for the causes of hysteria with his own self-analysis, and this brought him back to the years in Freiberg. The 41-year-old Freud, a husband and father with six young children to support, sought to unravel what in his own early childhood had made him a neurotic and a hysteric.

He suspected that his nannie in Freiberg had taught him about sex, and that this woman, rather than his father, was the cause of his own hysteria. The pinpointing of his nannie's role in his development led to other pertinent information and recollections. It emerges that this woman, as mentioned, had stolen from the Freuds, and his adult half-brother, Philipp, had turned her into the police and she was imprisoned. Her sudden disappearance from his life was unsettling to the young Sigismund. In a letter dated 15 October 1897 to his friend Fliess, he recalls how as a youngster he became worried that his mother might also vanish from him as his nannie just had. When he could not find his beloved mother, he thought Amalie might have been locked up too and he asked Philipp to unlock a wardrobe. When his mother was not there, Sigismund began crying and only settled down when his mother came into the house.

Having resolved to his own satisfaction the origination of his own hysteria and recognizing his own fear of loss of female attachment figures, Freud's self-analysis led him toward new and innovative conclusions. In the very next paragraph of the same letter, Freud makes one of his great leaps from a particular situation to a universal law:

A single idea of general value dawned on me. I have found, in my own case too, (the phenomenon of) being in love with my mother and jealous of my father, and now I consider it a universal event in early childhood. If this is so, we can understand the gripping power of *Oedipus Rex*...the Greek legend seizes upon a compulsion which everyone recognizes because he senses it within himself. Everyone in the audience was once a budding Oedipus in fantasy and each recoils in horror from the dream fulfillment here transplanted into reality with the full quantity of repression which separates his infantile state from his present one.

(Freud, 1985, p. 272)

And, thus, Freud has given birth to the Oedipus complex. There is both an important insight and an astounding leap in this new theory. How does Freud know that everyone was once a budding Oedipus? Clearly, this is based more on intuition than evidence. Besides his self-analysis, Freud bases his conclusions on literature and the case of one of his clients. In May 1897, Freud had discussed a boy's hostile impulses toward his father and a girl toward her mother. Now he is adding the element of love for the mother as the source of the boy's anger toward the father.

What gives this preliminary version of the Oedipus complex its power is its emphasis on the importance of the mother to the male child, the child's desire for exclusive possession, his fear of loss, his identifying the father as the reason he cannot have his mother, and his subsequent animosity toward the father. Freud recognizes that Oedipal desires, like seduction scenes, are repressed from memory, and gain their power from being unconscious.

In coming upon the elements of the Oedipus complex, as mentioned earlier, Freud is completing a shift of responsibility from the perversion of the parent to the fears and desires of the child. Freud is also moving from examining what engenders hysteria to generalizing about the human condition. Though he briefly resurrects the seduction thesis later in the year, he is turning from what is abnormal to what is universal. Still, as with his study of hysteria, Freud keeps his focus on the domestic sphere; but, unlike his views on hysteria, he emphasizes the universality of Oedipal phenomena. "It is the fate of all of us, perhaps, to direct our first sexual impulse towards our mother and our first hatred and our first murderous wish against our father" (Freud, 1953 [1900], *SE IV*, p. 262).

Fathers and Brothers

Yet this new theory raises as many questions as it answers. In the Oedipus complex, a universal nuclear family structure is assumed, with a mother-father-son triad at its core. Ironically, Freud came upon this complex, in large part, by analyzing his own family of origin in Freiberg, an extended family and household where an older half-brother and a nannie are as important as the mother and father. There is this peculiar disparity between Freud's original formulation of the Oedipus complex and the realities of his family life in Freiberg. English professor Madelon Sprengnether notices the difference between the Freiberg and Vienna Freuds. "The Oedipus complex, with its streamlined nuclear family structure, seems to be modeled on the family that reconstituted itself around Jacob, Amalie, and their children rather than the one that embraced Philipp, Emmanuel and Maria" (Sprengnether, 1990, p. 18).

The reasons for this odd disjuncture become clearer when Freud (1901), in *The Psychopathology of Everyday Life,* returns to the story of his mother, brother, and nurse that he first recounted in 1897 to Fliess. In 1901, he writes:

I saw myself standing in front of a cupboard... demanding something and screaming, while my half-brother held it open. Then suddenly my mother, looking beautiful and slim, walked into the room, as if she had come in from the street. These were the words in which I described the scene but I did not know what I could make of it. Analytic effort led me to take a quite unexpected view of the picture. I had missed my mother, and had come to suspect that she was shut up in this wardrobe or cupboard; and it was for that reason that I was demanding that my brother should open the cupboard... But how did the child get the idea of looking for his absent mother in the cupboard? Dreams which I had at the same ti.me [as the analysis of this memory] contained obscure allusions to a nurse of whom I had other recollections...this clever but dishonest person bad carried out considerable thefts in the house...and had been taken to court on a charge preferred by my half-brother...the reason why I had turned in particular to this brother...was probably because I bad noticed that he played a part in her disappearance; and he had answered in the elusive and punning fashion that was characteristic of him: 'She's boxed up'. At the time, I understood this answer m a child's way...When my mother left me a short while later, I suspected that my naughty brother bad done the same thing to her that he had done to the nurse and I forced him to open the cupboard...I now understood...why my mother's slimness was emphasized: it must have struck me as having just been restored to her. I am two and a half years older than the sister who was born at that time.

(Freud, 1960 [1901], *SE VI*, pp. 49–51)

Freud elaborates on the meaning of this story in a significant footnote added 23 years later. When in the 1901 account he had described his mother as slim and beautiful he saw this as meaning that his mother was not now pregnant. The young Sigmund had understood that his baby sister "had grown inside his mother." Young Sigmund suspected that his half-brother Philipp "had in some way introduced the recently born baby into his mother's inside" (Freud, 1960 [1901], *SE VI*, p. 51). If his brother had impregnated his mother, and Sigmund was afraid it could happen again, he had reason to be jealous of Philipp. In the same footnote Freud wrote: "His big brother…had taken his father's place as the child's rival" (Freud, 1960 [1901], *SE VI*, p. 51).

How can this be? A universal event in early childhood is love of the mother and jealousy of the father, and this is true in his own case. Freud had announced this in the same letter in which he had first recounted the wardrobe incident and announced the Oedipus complex. There was no mention then that a same-sex sibling could displace the father, or had done so in his own case. The Oedipus complex takes on a whole new meaning, if there are four players rather than three.

Freud's description of himself and his family dynamics do not fully match his description of the structure of the Oedipus complex. The actual father, who shares a bed with the mother, has been overthrown in the child's mind and a second father figure has been installed as the chief rival. Variations in family structure and dynamics resulted in variations in the child's psyche. How can the Oedipal triad be universal when it does not even apply in Freud's own case? Can the Oedipus complex be conceived of as a mother-father-child triad when a sibling can replace a parent as a rival? Furthermore, because of the role of Sigmund's half-brother, the Oedipus complex cannot be conceived as just desire for the mother and hostility toward the father. The Oedipal dynamic cannot be treated just as an isolated triangle separate from the rest of the family.

In 1916, Freud had written that when "other children appear on the scene the Oedipus complex is enlarged into a family complex" (Freud, 1963 [1916], *SE XVI*, p. 333). The "position of a child in the family order is a factor of extreme importance in determining the shape of his later life and should deserve consideration in every life-history" (Freud, 1963 [1916], *SE XVI*, p. 334). In Freud's own life, there is an unusual paradox relating to the family order. On the one hand, he is the oldest child living in a family and household with his mother and father. On the other hand, of the Freiberg Freuds, he is the youngest of the three sons of Jakob Freud, and his older half-brothers are so intimately a part of the family that Sigmund could consider a half-brother to be more of a rival for his mother's love than his actual father. The position of the child in the family order then has dramatic consequences for the shape the Oedipal dynamics take. In Freud's own case, his Oedipus complex is part and parcel of a family complex.

The child's desire for the mother remains the foundation for Oedipal dynamics. But to whom in the family the child's hostility is directed may vary. The relevant family cast of the Oedipal drama need not be just mother, father, and son, but includes other pertinent family actors, whether they dwell in the same abode or not. It may even include non-family members, such as Sigmund's nannie.

This discrepancy between the Oedipal triad and the larger family structure is very significant for understanding what the Oedipus complex entails. An essential component of Freud's conception of the Oedipus complex is the son's jealousy toward the father. But what happens to the Oedipus complex if the father is not the son's rival? This is a question that has been of significance to psychoanalysis since Malinowski. From its very inception, Freud himself confused the role of fathers and brothers in the Oedipus complex. As a result, it is uncertain what the Oedipus complex in its first formulation actually entailed, and if the concept of an Oedipal triangle of mother-father-child is adequate to explain the psychological dynamics Freud describes.

In his first published writings about the Oedipus complex, Freud gives the impression that the Oedipus complex is part of our biological inheritance. In 1900, as mentioned he writes that incestuous wishes toward the father are "forced upon us by Nature" (Freud, 1953 [1900], *SE IV*, p. 263). This gives the impression that the family has a uniform structure, and that the elementary family is a fact of nature. It is only after the First World War has begun that Freud even considers how the impact of other children in the family impacts upon the unfolding of the Oedipus complex. Variations in family structure and dynamics are not part of how Freud conceives of the Oedipus complex, even though they were crucial in his own development, and in how he came upon the notion of the Oedipus complex. Freud's formulation of the male Oedipal phenomena, with its emphasis on the parents-son triad, is a way of simplifying a very complicated family dynamic.

To recapitulate, Freud's conception of the Oedipus complex halts just as it is about to confront variations in family structure and dynamics, the very differences that Freud was intimately aware of from his own early family life. The Freud who discovered the Oedipus complex is simultaneously a bold investigator, an innovative theorist, and a man who hides certain things from himself. He reveals and conceals at the same time.

There is another irony here. Freud's discovery of the Oedipus complex was deeply connected to his own self-analysis. Late in life, Freud came to have doubts about the sufficiency of self-examination. In 1935, he writes: "In self-analysis the danger of incompleteness is particularly great. One is too soon satisfied with a part explanation, behind which resistance may easily be keeping back something that is more important perhaps" (Freud, 1964 [1935], *SE XXII*, p. 234).

If there are resistances in his own self-analysis, they might have to do with his fears about his half-brother's relationship to his mother and his difficulty facing his ambivalent feelings about his mother and women. The Oedipal son's anger, according to Freud, is directed toward the father. Would it not be equally aimed at a mother who chooses a father or an adult half-brother over the son? Freud does say that the son views the mother's intimacy with the father as a betrayal, but he does not integrate this into his conception of the dynamics of the Oedipus complex. It is understandable that Freud could be confounded by his contradictory feelings, and needed to keep some of them hidden from himself. This combination of discovery and denial makes it more difficult for Freud to carry to completion his self-analysis, and then to develop a coherent theory of the nature of the Oedipus complex.

Instead of examining the Oedipal triangle with the family complex, after his breaks with Adler and Jung, Freud's main tendency is to emphasize the role of biology in etiology. The deeper he gets into explaining how the Oedipus complex develops, the more he relies on a theory which does not need to take actual experiences into account. A way out of further examining how variations in family life impact upon the Oedipus complex is to have the unconscious mind reshape reality to fit its own categories. If the child's unconscious reduces the variations in family structure and positions to the Oedipal triad, then reality matters less than a pre-ordained mental structure. Freud turns to such a conception in his notion of the phylogenetic inheritance. Such a notion declares that no matter who nourishes the child, the imagination reformulates it to the mother, and whether or not the biological father is present, the phylogenetic inheritance has a father in the child's psyche. Triangular Oedipal dynamics are then preserved in the child's imagination. Freud's conception of our biological heritage eliminates the need to consider-how the actual experiences of the individual shape his or her complexes. Unfortunately, the phylogenetic inheritance does not explain how Sigmund's brother, Philipp, came to replace his father as Sigmund's chief rival for his mother. Freud presented the idea of the family complex, with its emphasis on experience, only a few years after promulgating his theories on the overriding impact of phylogeny.

In the Oedipal triangle, Freud claims to have found the neurotic core of the human psyche, the way that all youngsters are torn between desire and animosity. Nature rather than nurture appears to be the cause of humankind's emotional conflicts. Yet there are puzzles, gaps, and dilemmas that arise out of Freud's first conception of the Oedipus complex. Despite his efforts to give priority to biology, Freud's ideas on the etiology of the Oedipus complex remain divided between inherited and acquired factors. Freud, like the rest of us, is an individual whose inner divisions impact on his ability to develop a coherent and comprehensive theory. His failure to integrate the role of his older brother and the role of his father into his conception of the Oedipus complex leaves his theory incomplete and inconsistent with the evidence he presents. Given that there can be more than three parties to the Oedipus complex, it is not clear from Freud's writings what the Oedipus complex actually means, what it entails, and how it develops.

Freud, in searching for the root causes of his hysteria, examined the complexities of his extended family in Freiberg. When he represented the core conflicts of these early years, he needed to reduce what had been a series of entangled and interconnected dyads, triangles, and quartets into one essential drama between mother, son, and father. As an adult, he remained as confounded by the complications in his family constellation as he was as a young boy. A task of the intellectual descendants of Freud is to recover the multi-complexities of the family romance he both revealed and concealed, and to place the dynamics of the Oedipus complex within the full family context in which it unfolds.

References

Anzieu, D. (1986). *Freud's self-analysis*. The Hogarth Press and the Institute of Psycho-Analysis.

Beller, S. (1989). *Vienna and the Jews 1867–1938: A cultural history*. Cambridge University Press.

Bernays, A. F. (1940). My brother, Sigmund Freud. *American Mercury*, Volume 51, pp. 335–342.

Bettelheim, B. (1990). *Freud's Vienna and other essays*. Alfred A. Knopf.

Clark, R. (1980). *Freud: The man and his cause*. Random House.

Decker, H. (1991). *Freud, Dora and Vienna, 1900*. The Free Press.

Freud, M. (1958). *Freud, man and father.* Jason Aronson.

Freud, S. (1953). *The interpretation of dreams. The standard edition of the complete psychological works, SE IV* (J. Strachey Ed and Trans). The Hogarth Press (Original work published 1900).

Freud, S. (1953). *Three essays on the theory of sexuality. The standard edition of the complete psychological works, SE VII* (J. Strachey Ed and Trans). The Hogarth Press, pp. 125–248 (Original work published 1905).

Freud, S. (1955). *Totem and taboo, The standard edition of the complete psychological works, SE XIII* (J. Strachey Ed and Trans). The Hogarth Press, pp. 13–164 (Original work published 1913).

Freud, S. (1955). *Beyond the pleasure principle. The standard edition of the complete psychological works, SE XVIII* (J. Strachey Ed and Trans). The Hogarth Press, pp. 7–64 (Original work published 1920).

Freud, S. (1955). Two encyclopedia articles. *The standard edition of the complete psychological works, SE XVIII* (J. Strachey Ed and Trans). The Hogarth Press, pp. 233–259 (Original work published 1923).

Freud, S. (1959). *An autobiographical study. The standard edition of the complete psychological works, SE XX* (J. Strachey Ed and Trans). The Hogarth Press, pp. 7–74 (Original work published 1925).

Freud, S. (1959). *Inhibitions, symptoms, and anxiety. The standard edition of the complete psychological works, SE XX* (J. Strachey Ed and Trans). The Hogarth Press, pp. 77–178 (Original work published 1926).

Freud, S. (1960). *Letters of Sigmund Freud.* Basic Books.

Freud, S. (1960). *The psychopathology of everyday life. The standard edition of the complete psychological works, SE VI* (J. Strachey Ed and Trans). The Hogarth Press (Original work published 1901).

Freud, S. (1961). Female sexuality. *The standard edition of the complete psychological works, SE XXI* (J. Strachey Ed and Trans). The Hogarth Press, pp. 225–243 (Original work published 1931).

Freud, S. (1962). Screen memories. *The standard edition of the complete psychological works, SE III* (J. Strachey Ed and Trans). The Hogarth Press, pp. 301–322 (Original work published 1899).

Freud, S. (1963). *Introductory lectures on psycho-analysis. The standard edition of the complete psychological works, SE XVI* (J. Strachey Ed and Trans). The Hogarth Press (Original work published 1916).

Freud, S. (1964). *New introductory lectures on psycho-analysis. The standard edition of the complete psychological works, SE XXII* (J. Strachey Ed and Trans). The Hogarth Press (Original work published 1933).

Freud, S. (1964). The subtleties of a faulty action. *The standard edition of the complete psychological works, SE XXII* (J. Strachey Ed and Trans). The Hogarth Press, pp. 233–238 (Original work published 1935).

Freud, S. (1964). *An outline of psycho-analysis. The standard edition of the complete psychological works, SE XXIII* (J. Strachey Ed and Trans). The Hogarth Press, pp. 141–204 (Original work published 1940).

Freud, S. (1985). *The complete letters of Sigmund Freud to Wilhelm Fliess.* Harvard University Press.

Gay, P. (1988). *Freud: A life for our time.* W. W. Norton & Company.

Heller, J. B. (1956). Freud's mother and father. *Commentary*, Volume 21, pp. 418–421.

Jones, E. (1953). *Sigmund Freud: Life and work, Vol. 1, The young Freud: 1856–1900.* The Hogarth Press.

Kitcher, P. (1992). *Freud's dream: A complete interdisciplinary science of mind.* MIT Press.

Krull, M. (1986). *Freud and his father.* W. W. Norton & Company.

Oxaal, I., and Weitzmann, W. (1985). The Jews of pre-1914 Vienna: an exploration of basic sociological dimensions. *Leo Baeck Yearbook*, Volume 30, pp. 395–432.

Sprengnether, M. (1990). *The spectral mother: Freud, feminism, and psychoanalysis.* Cornell University Press.

Wistrich, R. (1990). *The Jews of Vienna in the age of Franz Joseph.* Oxford University Press.

Young-Bruehl, E. (1988). *Anna Freud: A biography.* Summit Books.

Chapter 3

The Evolution of Freud's View of Parental/Paternal Authority

There are still additional factors to consider in relation to Freud fathers, sons, and paternal authority. Freud proclaims that the rebellion against paternal rule is always present in sons, if not always daughters. Freud's vacillations on the role of parental/paternal authority are evidence of how his internal divisions impacted on his outlook. His attitudes toward paternal/parental authority did evolve. At times, the early Freud appears to be sympathetic to a rebellion against authority. In 1905, Freud declares,

> one of the most painful, psychical achievements of the pubertal period is completed: detachment from parental authority, a process that alone makes possible the opposition, which is so important for the progress of civilization, between the new generation and the old.
>
> (Freud, 1953 [1905], SE VII, p. 227)

Four years later, he declares: "the whole progress of society rests upon the opposition between successive generations" (Freud, 1959 [1909], SE IX, p. 237). The youngster recognizes the parents' limitations and inadequacies. The "child's imagination becomes engaged in the task of getting free from the parents of whom he now has such a low opinion" (Freud, 1959 [1909], SE IX, p. 238). This struggle for emancipation is gender based. A "boy is far more inclined to feel hostile impulses towards his father than towards his mother and has a more intense desire to get free from *him* than from *her*" (Freud, 1959 [1909], SE X, p. 238). This wish for autonomy to Freud is not only inevitable; it is desirable. "The liberation of an individual, as he grows up, from the authority of his parents is one of the most necessary though one of the most painful results brought about by the course of his development" (Freud, 1959 [1909], SE X, p. 237).

This is a somewhat liberal Freud, siding with the underlings against authority, and championing the autonomy of the individual. According to Weinstein and Platt, Freud's "demand for the liberation of the ego can be seen as one step in the process that began with the Protestant Reformation" (Weinstein and Platt, 1969, p. 153). However, just when Freud appears to be laying down the gauntlet for a battle of generations, he pulls back. He reassures the reader that these rebellions

DOI: 10.4324/9781041074717-5

"still preserve, under a slight disguise, the child's original affection for his parents. The faithlessness and ingratitude are only apparent" (Freud, 1959 [1909], SE X, p. 240). The "whole effort at replacing the real father by a superior one is only" a "turning away from the father whom he knows to-day to the father in whom he believed in the earlier years of his childhood; and...a regret that those happy days have gone" (Freud, 1959 [1909], SE X, pp. 240–241). What began as an affirmation that society's progress depends upon the conflict of generations ends up as a nostalgic affirmation of the child's gratitude toward his parents. His 1909 article, "Family Romances," shows how the Oedipal rebellion is rooted not only in the jealousies of the son, but the imperfection of the parents.

Freud's pattern of both rebellion against and loyalty to paternal authority echoes the cycle of the modern liberal tradition of rebellion against and affirmation of social authority. From Luther's Protestant Reformation to the New Left and counter-culture of the 1960s, rebellion has been a periodically recurring phenomenon in the West. This tradition of revolt has taken a variety of forms, from the political, to the literary, to the cultural, to the familial. For all its variation, there has been a repeated pattern of rebellion followed by acquiescence, and often later an affirmation of the very things against which one rebelled. This repeated pattern in modern Western history is a product of divided loyalties, and a reversal of perspectives. What was once championed is often discarded, what was rejected is later affirmed.

Sigmund Freud's own route did go from affirming the perspective of the son to defending paternal authority. It is an example of this pattern. After the defection of Adler and the conflict with Jung. Freud's perspective on rebellion and fathers changed. He identified less as the son and more as the father against whom the son's death wishes were aimed. With this change of perspective, his attitude toward authority began to alter. There was less emphasis on the son's justified reasons for rebelling against the father, gone was the notion that society's progress depended on the opposition between the generations. Over time, the father emerged as the bearer of the severe authority of the super-ego. The image of the father in the later Freud is of a tyrannical, punitive, castrating figure. What is later underplayed in Freud's thought is that the father's ordinary human faults can justify the son's revolt against paternal authority. Though Freud still emphasizes the inevitability of male intergenerational conflict, the results are not progress, but the reaffirmation of the rule of the father.

This shift in Freud's self-identification is evident in *Totem and Taboo*, published in 1913. Freud postulates a primal horde, ruled by a tyrannical father who maintains a sexual monopoly over all the women. The lustful but deprived sons join together, murder, and devour the father in order to gain sexual access to the females. Once the primal crime has been completed, the brothers feel guilt and remorse over these terrible actions against their own flesh and blood. The

tumultuous mob of brothers were filled with the...contradictory feelings...at work in the ambivalent father-complexes of our children....They hated their father... but they loved and admired him too. After they had got rid of him, had satisfied their hatred and had put into effect their wish to identify themselves with him, the affection which had all this time been pushed under was bound to make itself felt. It did so in the form of remorse. A sense of guilt made its appearance.

(Freud, 1959 [1913], SE XIII, p. 143)

The result, according to Freud's account, was a belated form of filial piety. What previously the father's rule had prevented "was thenceforth prohibited by the sons themselves, in accordance with the psychological procedure so familiar to us... under the name of 'deferred obedience'" (Freud, 1959 [1913], SE XIII, p. 143). They forbid further killing of fathers and father substitutes and renounced their claims to the women. "They thus created out of their filial sense of guilt the two fundamental taboos...that...correspond to the two repressed wishes of the Oedipus complex" (Freud, 1959 [1913], SE XIII, p. 143).

There are clearly parallels between Freud's myth in *Totem and Taboo* and his earlier accounts of rebellion. In the earlier period, disappointment and need for self-development motivate the action; in the later version, hatred of the father and a desire to have his power led the brothers to kill their father. In "Family Romances," rebellion led to social progress. In *Totem and Taboo*, patricide results not in liberation, but in deferred obedience to paternal authority. Freud the father is proclaiming that no matter how extreme their hostile actions, sons cannot escape their subservience to the internalized father. The conservative Freud, the one who stresses the inevitability of patriarchy, is beginning to make his appearance.

A few years later, in 1918, Freud adopts a doctrine that shows how sons inevitably fear their fathers. A phylogenetic inheritance derived from humankind's prehistory is the fate of all humans. These

phylogenetic inherited schemata...are concerned with the business of 'placing' the impressions derived from actual experience....The Oedipus complex, which comprises a child's relation to his parents, is...the best known member of the class. Whenever experience fails to fit in with the hereditary schema, they become remodeled in the imagination.

(Freud, 1955 [1918], SE XVII, p. 119)

In the above passage, Freud is referring to the case of the Wolf-Man, where threats of castration toward him emanated from women. Nevertheless, "it was his father from whom he came to fear castration. In this respect, heredity triumphed over accidental experience; in man's prehistory it was unquestionably the father who practiced castration as a punishment" (Freud, 1955 [1918], SE XVII, p. 86).

The punitive father-image is now part of everyone's biological inheritance, no matter what happens in a person's own life. The earlier Freud had society's progress and individual emancipation from parental authority going hand-in-hand. This later Freud sees history as a repeating cycle where individual experience must fit into a pre-determined psychological pattern that brings terror of the father and deferred obedience to paternal authority.

Freud develops the doctrine of the super-ego in the 1920s and 1930s. This concept reinforces the continuity of authority from the familial father to the political patriarchy. The super-ego, Freud says, emerges as the Oedipus complex comes to a resolution. As with so much of Freud, he applies the concept of the super-ego more to males than females and is concerned once again with the power relationship of fathers and sons. The Oedipus complex develops during the phallic stage, when the child has increased genital sensations. It is then that the male child perceives his father as a rival for his mother and becomes jealous and hostile. When he sees a female nude, according to Freudian theory, the boy becomes aware of her absence of a penis and to him, the girl is castrated. The boy then begins to fear castration from his own father, either in reality or from the phylogenetically inherited schema. To preserve himself, the son renounces desire for his mother and internalizes the father's prohibitions. The Oedipus complex dissolves, the super-ego rules, and the authority of the father is carried on from generation to generation. Freud's presentation of the super-ego is two sided: "the super-ego… represents demands of a restrictive and rejecting character….repression is the work of this super-ego" (Freud, 1964 [1932], SE XXII, p. 69). Then again: "The super-ego is the representative for us of every moral restriction, the advocate of a striving towards perfection-it is, in short…what is described as the higher side of human life" (Freud, 1964 [1932], SE XXII, pp. 66–67). There is a side of the super-ego that enforces punishments for violating injunctions and there is a side of the super-ego that embodies the highest values. The super-ego has "the functions of self-observation, of conscience and of [maintaining] the ideal" (Freud, 1964 [1932], SE XXII, p. 66).

How this part of the mind combines both sides is not clear. What is definite is that the super-ego in its prohibitive and idealistic functions is connected to the parents, in general, and the father, in particular. "The super-ego….preserves throughout life the character given to it by its derivation from the father-complex" (Freud, 1961 [1923], SE XIX, p. 48). The "origin of the ego-ideal" is in "an individual's first and most important identification with the father in his own personal prehistory" (Freud, 1961 [1923], SE XIX, p. 31). "The super-ego arises…from an identification with the father taken as a model" (Freud, 1961 [1923], SE XIX, p. 54). As it develops, the "super-ego retains the character of the father" and takes "the form of conscience or perhaps of an unconscious sense of guilt" (Freud, 1961 [1923], SE XIX, pp. 34–35). It does so by combining a positive and a negative: it says: "You *ought to be* like this (like your father)"; it also comprises the prohibition: "You *may not be* like this (like your father), that is, you may not do all that he does; some things are his prerogative" (Freud, 1961 [1923], SE XIX, p. 34).

With this doctrine of the super-ego, Freud has completed his conception of the cycle of the Oedipus complex. It begins in identification with the father, goes through a period of rivalry toward the father in the phallic stage, and is completed when the son renounces desire for the mother and rebellion against the father, adopts the father's values, and defers to his authority. Rebellion against the father is just a stage.

The implication is that continuing to challenge paternal authority is a sign of an unresolved Oedipus complex. Obedience to the authority of the father following the period of rebellion shows a successful resolution of the Oedipus complex, and an ability to go on to the next stage of development. Progress and normal development now are tied to the son's internalization of the father's super-ego injunctions. This contrasts with Freud's earlier declarations that "liberation" from "the authority of the parents" is "quite essential" and "has been to some extent achieved by everyone who has reached a normal state" (Freud, 1959 [1909], SE X, p. 237). The transition from the liberal to the conservative Freud and the conservative super-ego has been completed.

While Freud overtly proclaims internal conformity to the super-ego paternal authority, he is often better able to do it in theory than in practice. As Otto Rank pointed out Freud was "a rebellious son who defends paternal authority" (Rank, 1930, p. 191). Freud's divided self between demanding doctrinal obedience but somehow enabling other sons to rebel as he had done has been a pattern not only of Freud's but of the rifts within psychoanalysis down to the present day. Many other leaders of movements have been sufficiently internally resolved as to have followers who followed every command of the paternal authority. This was not the psychic reality for Freud himself and within the psychoanalytic movement. His own uncertainty between rebellion and obedience somehow allowed others to dissent rather than to honor the psychoanalytic founder and father. Sigmund Freud was unable to effectively communicate deference to his authority given his unresolved conflicts between being son and father. This Freudian uncertainty was present in himself and in the internally conflicted doctrines of much of what this great innovator promulgated. It is also evident when Freud first became the father figure/the authority in the Vienna Psychoanalytic Society.

References

Freud, S. (1953). *The standard edition of the complete psychological works Vol. VII* (J. Strachey Ed. and Trans.). The Hogarth Press (Original work published 1905).

Freud, S. (1955). *The standard edition of the complete psychological works Vol. VII* (J. Strachey Ed. and Trans.). The Hogarth Press (Original work published 1905).

Freud, S. (1955). *The standard edition of the complete psychological works Vol. XVII* (J. Strachey Ed. and Trans.). The Hogarth Press (Original work published 1918).

Freud, S. (1959). *The standard edition of the complete psychological works Vol. IX* (J. Strachey, Ed. and Trans.). The Hogarth Press (Original work published in 1909).

Freud, S. (1959). *The standard edition of the complete psychological works Vol. XIII* (J. Strachey Ed. and Trans.). The Hogarth Press (Original work published 1913).

Freud, S. (1961). *The standard edition of the complete psychological works Vol. XIX* (J. Strachey Ed. and Trans.). The Hogarth Press (Original work published 1923).

Freud, S. (1964). *The standard edition of the complete psychological works Vol. XXII* (J. Strachey Ed. and Trans.). The Hogarth Press (Original work published 1932).

Rank, O. (1930). *Modern education.* New York, NY: Alfred A. Knopf.

Weinstein, F. and Platt, G. (1969). *The wish to be free: Society, psyche, and value change.* University of California Press.

Chapter 4

Freud and the Vienna Psychoanalytic Society

The first surviving evidence of psychoanalysis as a 'scientific' movement comes from the Vienna Psychoanalytic Society. It is here where there is a concrete example of how Freud's internal splits between being the father, the sibling, and the son become evident. For squabbles and schisms befell this group, and were a result in part of the unconscious mixed messages Freud gave his followers. Clearly conflicts erupted between Freud and his Viennese followers at the Psychoanalytic Conference at Nuremberg in 1910 and then back in Vienna during the next year. Revisiting the reasons for these tensions helps clarify the character of Freud's leadership and the evolution of the psychoanalytic movement. The documentation of these early days is in the recorded minutes of the Vienna Psychoanalytic Society from 1906 to 1918, Freud's letters and writings, and the memoirs of various participants.

There is an account of Viennese Psychoanalysis by one of Freud's early, but now obscure, followers. This is the 2005 translation of the 1930 memoirs of Viennese neurologist Isidor Sadger (1867–1942), entitled *Recollecting Freud*. As Rosencrantz to Freud's Hamlet, Sadger plays a minor role in the psychoanalytic drama. Yet his reflections as seconded by others add to our understanding of Freud and the course of psychoanalysis.

Much of what Sadger says in his memoir about Freud is highly critical. Freud is also disparaging of Sadger. Not surprisingly, Freud's adherents are not Sadger admirers. Vincent Brome writes that Freudian loyalist, Ernest Jones, after becoming familiar with Sadger's books, suggested in the 1930s that Sadger "should be put in a concentration camp" (Brome, 1983, p. 186). Sadger in September 1942 was sent to the Theresienstadt concentration camp, and died there that December (Handlbauer, 1998, p. 38).

In an earlier time, Sadger was one of the first to recognize Freud's significance. As Alan Dundes writes: "In sheer terms of hours spent in the presence of Freud… Sadger had few peers" (Dundes, 2005, p. xxxvii). In 1895, Sadger began attending Freud's lectures at the University of Vienna; this was before Freud published the seduction theory and prior to Sigmund's self-analysis. Sadger was an active member of the Viennese Psychoanalytic Society from 1906 to 1933. Between 1906 and 1918, Sadger made 20 presentations to the Society, which is more than anyone else. Stekel gave 15 presentations, Freud 12, and Adler 11 (Nunberg and Federn, 1962).

DOI: 10.4324/9781041074717-6

Freud's biographer, and former member of the Vienna Psychoanalytic Society, Fritz Wittels, writes in 1924 that "Sadger was the first who made use of psychoanalysis for the cure of homosexuality" and "was the first to recognize that narcissism belongs to the same order of phenomena as homosexuality" (Wittels, 1924, pp. 213–214). Bernhard Handlbauer believes that Sadger "belongs to the pioneers of early psychoanalysis" (Handlbauer, 1998, p. 38.). However, the editor of Sadger's recollections, anthropologist Alan Dundes, maintains that "most histories of psychoanalysis rarely or barely mention him" (Dundes, 2005, p. xix).

Whether or not he was a psychoanalytic pioneer, the response of Freud and others to Sadger reveals much about how the Viennese followers of Freud conducted themselves. Sadger's talks before the Vienna Psychoanalytic Society, as Dundes documents, aroused controversy. Freud and others severely criticized Sadger's ideas, manner, and character. For example, after a presentation of Sadger's at the Society on December 4, 1907, Freud declared that Sadger "has a rigidly established way of working," he "too often expended" his industry "on sterile topics," and that "there is altogether no need to write such pathographies" as Sadger is wont to do (Nunberg and Federn, 1962, Vol. 1, p. 257). In comments following a Sadger talk before the Society on May 5, 1909, Freud said Sadger's work "seems to be wholly unreliable" and is "a complete failure." Sadger's "communications feel strange to us, sometimes even offensive....Sadger must also be reproached for having a special predilection for the brutal." There is a "lack of tolerance" in Sadger's approach which "manifests itself in a moralistic pathos" which Freud finds to be "repellent" (Nunberg and Federn, 1962, Vol. 2, pp. 224–225). Freud, at a January 5, 1910, meeting, said he had a response of "antagonism" to Sadger's presentation. One reason for this response exists "in the speaker himself" for giving an "overwhelming mass of details" rather than just "presenting only the results." Sadger also takes as proven what "are still matters for debate" (Nunberg and Federn, Vol. 2, 1962, p. 379).

Sadger did not react kindly to the critical remarks made on his content and manner. After the December 1907 discussion of his paper, he complained about the "personal insults" and "invectives" directed toward him (Nunberg and Federn, Vol. 1, 1962, p. 258). At a February 5, 1908 meeting of the Society, Sadger made a motion proposing: "Personal invectives and attacks should immediately be suppressed by the Chairman." Freud was "opposed" to this motion as he favored an individual being able to express "his true scientific opinion" (Nunberg and Federn, 1962, Vol. 1, pp. 300–301). The motion did not pass.

In characterizing as real scientific discussion what were also ad hominem attacks, Freud enabled the continuation of personal invective. Freud himself clearly was not reticent about personally disparaging Sadger and finding his talks repellent. The leader, Dr Freud, vented his personal antagonism to Sadger, rather than sticking solely to intellectual issues. Often at these meetings, issues of content and personality were intermixed. Searching for criteria to evaluate whether claims were scientific was not always front and center.

Sadger's memoirs show Freud as a creative genius but also as a leader who permits discourteous comments and tries to dominate his followers.

In *Recollecting Freud*, Sadger says that that lack of friendly relations among the group members was somewhat Freud's fault. He could have "kept a tight rein on the students" and made "crucial interventions." On occasion, though, Sadger writes, Freud "presented a bad example to the others. How could he press for courteous friendliness and halt every attack that was not purely factual if he himself blithely disregarded both rules and to be sure, did so more than once" (Sadger, 2005, p. 42).

Freud allowed himself the freedom to criticize others, but was not always tolerant when his own doctrines came under the analytic microscope. According to Sadger, Freud demanded conformity to his own ideas. "Freud," Sadger declares, "was not merely the father of psychoanalysis, but also its tyrant!" (Sadger, 2005, p, 40). Freud was not pleased if one of "his followers "wanted to discover something on his own" (Sadger, 2005, p. 39). He "was not free of envy of his most talented disciples, if they even once found something new....his strong narcissism...required loudly articulated admiration" (Sadger, 2005, p. 55).

Some of Freud's adherents, Sadger says, "disavowed their own individuality" (Sadger, 2005, p. 40). Yet loyalty to Freud was not sufficient. "I was absolutely convinced that none of the closest students would be able to remain in a trouble-free harmonious relationship with the Professor for a lifetime" (Sadger, 2005, p. 36). For those "who stood closest to his emanations could not keep their limbs unscathed" (Sadger, 2005, p. 40). Since

> Freud could not for various weighty reasons show his displeasure to his opponents, he might on occasion let it break out against his own followers....a lightning bolt could suddenly come out of the blue and seriously injure the most loyal.
>
> (Sadger, 2005, pp. 42–43)

To Sadger, these attacks against his disciples came not only from Freud's frustrations, but his character. Sadger writes: "For Freud deep down inside was a terrible sadist which cost his enemies less than his students and most loyal followers. None of those who stood near him...would be spared the boot, sooner or later" (Sadger, 2005, p. 35).

As an example of Freud generating discord among his followers, Sadger discusses the psychoanalytic Congress at Nuremberg in March 1910. Freud without "first informing anyone" gave his Viennese followers "a frightful surprise." Freud had Ferenczi propose that Jung become President of the Psychoanalytic Association for life and be given veto power over publications. This was a "full-fledged dispossession and neglect of the Vienna school in favor of Jung" (Sadger, 2005, p. 75). Freud had set one group of psychoanalysts against another. The Viennese made a loud outcry against this Freudian favoritism. Freud subsequently retreated from his initial proposal and settled for a compromise that would allow an uneasy truce between the Austrians and the Swiss, one that would not give such concentrated powers to President Jung or give him a life term.

In the year following the Nuremberg Conference, the first schism in psychoanalysis occurred. There was controversy over the views of Alfred Adler and extensive discussion of his views at the Society's meetings in 1911. Freud made clear his displeasure with Adler's new ideas. The Society's minutes for February 22, 1911, have Freud saying: "Adler's doctrines" are "wrong and, as far as the development of psychoanalysis is concerned, dangerous" (Nunberg and Federn, 1962, Vol. 3, p. 172). In response to these criticisms and other maneuvers by Freud, Adler, but not all his followers, resigned from the Society, and Adler started another group. Some people belonged to both organizations. At the October 11, 1911 meeting of the Society, Freud says those who belong to "Dr. Adler's circle" are engaged in "hostile competition" and asks Adler's followers "to decide between membership either here or there" for being in both groups is "contradictory" (Nunberg and Federn, 1962, Vol. 3, p. 281). A resolution declaring that membership in the Vienna Psychoanalytic Society and Adler's group is "incompatible" passed and Adler's remaining followers resigned (Nunberg and Federn, 1962, Vol. 3, pp. 282–283). The purge was successful. Freud enforced doctrinal uniformity to his own views.

Sadger was not alone in criticizing Freud among the participants in the Vienna Psychoanalytic Society. Max Graf, an early member of the Society, wrote Freud "insisted that there was but one theory" and "if one followed Adler...one was no more a Freudian" (Graf, 1942, p. 473). For Freud "permitted no deviations from his orthodox teaching....When the question of his science came up, he would break with his most intimate and reliable friends" (Graf, 1942, pp. 471–472).

Wilhelm Stekel, the follower of Freud who had suggested that Freud hold the Wednesday night meetings, was worried "that any deviation from Freud constituted an act of rebellion. Such an attitude would not be in keeping with the idea of freedom of science" (Stekel, 1950, p. 141). Another early follower, Fritz Wittels, said Freud "has become a despot who will not tolerate the slightest deviation from his doctrine" (Wittels, 1924, p. 18). Wittels wrote that Freud "repels his friends and especially if they are men of importance" (Wittels, 1995, p. 139).

Even the loyal Hans Sachs, another member of the Society, said of Freud that "it was always extremely difficult for him to assimilate the opinions of others" (Sachs, 1944, p, 12). Sachs, speaking about Adler, wrote that Freud "did not spare his opponent and was not afraid of using sharp words and cutting remarks" (Sachs, 1944, p. 51). For Freud was "hard and sharp like steel, a 'good hater' close to the limit of vindictiveness" (Sachs, 1944, p. 115). Max Graf writes "we may think of" Freud "as a Moses full of wrath" (Graf, 1942, p. 472). Theodor Reik declares that Freud "was capable of much love, but he was also a good hater" (Reik, 1940, p. 6).

Of the members of the Vienna Psychoanalytic Society through 1918 who later recalled Freud, it was only Reik who viewed Freud as being "receptive to all new ideas and original thought in psychoanalysis" (Reik, 1940, p. 39). Reik though did not participate in the Society until after Adler and his followers had left.

There is evidence in Freud's letters that he sought conformity to his doctrines. As early as November 1909, Freud wrote to Jung about establishing a "literary dictatorship" in psychoanalytic publications (Freud and Jung, 1974, p. 260). Before the 1910 Nuremberg Conference, Freud described a paper of Adler's as "heretical" (Freud and Jung, 1974, p. 301). After Adler withdrew from the Society in 1911, Freud wrote that he needed to be careful so "that heresy does not occupy too much space" in psychoanalytic publications. In the same letter, he praised a follower for being "quite orthodox" (Freud and Jung, 1974, p. 400). In 1909, Freud wrote: "I sometimes get so angry at my Viennese that I wish…I could thrash them all with one stick" (Freud and Jung, 1974, p. 260).

Yet Freud's efforts to stamp out heresy and impose authoritarian rule were not altogether successful, and some of this was due to his own actions. After the Nuremberg Conference, on April 12, 1910, Freud wrote: "Fair competition between Vienna and Zurich can only benefit the cause" (Freud and Jung, 1974, p. 306). Nine days earlier, Freud had told Ferenczi of "my aversion toward the Viennese circle" (Freud and Ferenczi, 1993, p. 155). There was less fairness of competition than favoritism on Freud's part for Zurich. Sadger claimed that Freud had "a perpetual need for favorite students" (Sadger, 2005, p. 55).

Freud's playing off Zurich and Vienna, and enabling conflict among the Viennese boomeranged on him. After Nuremberg, he admitted to Ferenczi he had been "shortsighted" in not "sufficiently taking into account the effect this would have on the Viennese" (Freud and Ferenczi, 1993, p. 155). Freud by setting one group against another helped unleash resentments and conflict that led to schisms, defections, and bitterness. For Freud acted more like a competitive older brother, a rebellious son projecting the father role onto followers, and a wrathful father, rather than a benevolent father who brings the family together through his love and caring. The splits within psychoanalysis harmed the reputation of the movement as a scientific enterprise. The way factional conflicts evolved was, in part, a product of Freud's style of leadership.

E. James Lieberman, Otto Rank's biographer, concluded: "From 1911 on, intellectual independence in Freud's circle had to be subordinated to orthodoxy" (Lieberman, 1985, p. 127). To some, in the early psychoanalytic movement, there was less free scientific inquiry than a contentious group resembling a religious movement. As early as 1940, Reik had written that "psychoanalysts were called a sect" and "reproached" for "narrow-mindedness and dogmatism" (Reik, 1940, p. 36). Former Freudian, Max Graf, had written in 1942 of the meetings of Freud's followers: "There was an atmosphere of the foundation of a religion….Freud himself was its new prophet" and "Freud's pupils…were his apostles….he permitted no deviations from his orthodox teaching" (Graf, 1942, p. 471).

Some sectarian leaders are successful at retaining the loyalty and adherence of their disciples and others are not. Freud seems to fall more into the latter category. As early as 1924, Wittels had commented on the falling out Freud had with Breuer, Jung, Adler, and Stekel (Wittels, 1924, p. 114). Wittels does not mention Fliess, and later, of course, Rank would leave the fold, and there would be tension with Ferenczi. In interpersonal conflicts it takes two to tango. Still, it is hard not to recall Sadger's comments about Freud enacting his hostility on his followers rather than his opponents. Though Freud maintained for years strong relationships with many followers, the history of psychoanalysis is riddled with schisms.

Why did Freud's attempts at stamping out heresy run into so many roadblocks? Part of the answer lies in Freud's character. He was not successful as the tyrant, because he did not fully believe in his own authority. After the Nuremberg Conference but before the final confrontation with Adler, Freud wrote Jung that he is "torn" and has "fear of being regarded as an intolerant old man who holds the young men down, and this makes me feel uncomfortable" (Freud and Jung, 1974, p. 376). Otto Rank, as previously cited, captured Freud's internal divisions when we wrote the "founder" of psychoanalysis "is a rebellious son who defends the paternal authority, a revolutionary who, from fear of his own rebellious son-ego, took refuge in the security of the father position" (Rank, 1932, pp. 191–192). Freud was caught between being the father, the competitive brother, and the rebellious son. He enacted all three parts simultaneously, and could not consistently sustain belief in his role as supreme father figure. Freud recognized that "to excel one's father was still forbidden" and "a sense of guilt is attached to the satisfaction of having gone such a long way" (Freud, 1964 [1936], SE XXII, p. 247). Freud, unable to maintain the father's role with a clear conscience, reenacted father-son-sibling dramas with his followers. He alternated between the three roles, and projected all three parts on to his disciples-rivals-rebels.

As Sadger maintains, Freud at the meetings of the Vienna Psychoanalytic Society acted as a tyrant and enabler of sibling rivalry. There was a confusion of generations within Freud's psyche. Historian William McGrath comments on "the frequency of brother-father substitutions" in Freud's writings about himself (McGrath, 1986, p. 61). Psychoanalyst Leonard Shengold discusses how in Freud "hostility toward the father" is "displaced onto brother figures" (Shengold, 1993, p. 38). Sachs wrote of Freud: "Conflicts were an intrinsic part of his life" (Sachs, 1944, p. 110). Freud admitted: "My emotional life has always insisted that I should have an intimate friend and a hated enemy….it has not infrequently happened… that friend and enemy have come together in a single individual" (Freud, 1953 [1900], SE V, p. 483). This friend-combatant relationship is a sibling conflict containing a displacement of the rivalry with the father. Things become more complicated when the rebellious son, Sigmund, wants the father's authority.

Freud desires to be the father-dictator of psychoanalysis and yet feels guilty over suppressing the younger generation. He also identifies with the son's quest for independence from the father. But surpassing the father is forbidden. Freud was caught in a circle of conflicting identifications and counter-identifications. As the founding father of psychoanalysis, he could draw disciples, but in his conduct promoted both deference and rebellion. Certain followers wrestled with Freud and then left the fold. Freud's own psychic conflicts contributed to the divisions that have marked the history of psychoanalysis.

There are some additional wrinkles to this drama. Caught up in these generational confusions, Freud could not quite give sibling-sons their legitimate place, and therefore could not easily allow independent criteria to be established by which to judge psychoanalytic claims. Uncertain of his own place, he would not permit his doctrines to be evaluated for reliability and validity. Freudian psychoanalysis was too often as much a sect as a science. Concerns about the absence of appropriate intellectual standards have haunted the movement from Freud's time to the Freud Wars of the late 20th century.

There is another irony. In the fights with his followers, Freud received intellectual stimulus that enhanced his own theoretical development. Freud both identified with and against his disciples. He both rejected and internalized their ideas. The once rejected views germinated within him, his apparent rejection of his followers' ideas followed a strange internal path. Years later, without acknowledgment, he would often incorporate with modifications some of the ideas he had once vehemently opposed. Adler's unacceptable ideas on the importance of aggression and ego psychology years later became cornerstones of Freudian psychoanalysis. Stekel writes: "Freud later adopted some of my discoveries without mentioning my name....I had defined anxiety as the reaction of the *life instinct* against the upsurge of the *death instinct,*" yet this "was not mentioned" by Freud "in his later books" (Stekel, 1950, p. 138). Freud also incorporated some of Jung's ideas. Freud's creativity contained a complicated internal dialogue with the views of his former followers.

Freud clearly often developed his theories in response to the ideas of others. He often needed someone to play off of. He was a complex character. One side of Freud was torn between acting like a Moses type father to competitive siblings, another is later adopting perspectives he had earlier dismissed. His inner vacillations are often on display in the Vienna society. His inconsistent leadership fueled the conflicts and schisms that characterized psychoanalysis during and long after Freud's life. His internal conflicts over fathers, siblings, and sons, and his contradictory rejecting then affirming what he had disparaged have left a paradoxical impact on the history of psychoanalysis. His divided personal self was also reflected in his psychoanalytic theories.

It is clear in all four chapters in part one that Freud was a divided soul personally. Much of it had to do with fathers, sons, and siblings. These psychological divisions had a strong impact on how he developed and supported his doctrines. As such, his legacy to psychoanalysis was profound, mixed, and contradictory.

References

Brome, V. (1983). *Ernest Jones: A biography.* W.W. Norton & Company.

Dundes, A. (2005). Introduction. *Recollecting Freud* (I. Sadger Ed.). University of Wisconsin Press, pp. vii–lvii.

Freud, S. (1953). *The standard edition of the complete psychological works of Sigmund Freud, Volume V.* (J. Strachey Ed. and Trans.). The Hogarth Press (Original work published 1900).

Freud, S. (1964). A disturbance of memory on the acropolis. In J. Strachey (Ed. & Trans.), *The standard edition of the complete psychological works of Sigmund Freud, Volume XXII,* pp. 239–248. The Hogarth Press (Original work published 1936).

Freud, S. and Ferenczi, S. (1993). *The correspondence of Sigmund Freud and Sandor Ferenczi, Volume 1, 1908–1914* (E. Brabant, E. Falzeder, P. Giampieri-Deutsch Eds.). Harvard University Press.

Freud, S. and Jung, C. G. (1974). *The Freud/Jung letters: The correspondence between Sigmund Freud and C.G. Jung* (W. McGuire Ed.; R. Manheim, R. Hull Trans.). Princeton University Press.

Graf, M. (1942). Reminiscences of Professor Sigmund Freud. *Psychoanalytic Quarterly,* 11, pp. 465–476.

Handlbauer, B. (1998). *The Freud-Adler controversy.* One World.

Lieberman, E. J. (1985). *Acts of will: The life and work of Otto Rank.* The Free Press.

McGrath, W. (1986). *Freud's discovery of psychoanalysis.* Cornell University Press.

Nunberg, H. and Federn, E. (Eds.). (1962–1975). *Minutes of the Vienna Psychoanalytic Society, Volumes I-IV.* International Universities Press.

Rank, O. (1932). *Modern education.* Alfred A. Knopf.

Reik, T. (1940). *From thirty years with Freud.* International Universities Press.

Sachs, H. (1944). *Freud: Master and friend.* Imago Publishing Company.

Sadger, I. (2005). *Recollecting Freud* (J. Jacobsen; A. Dundes Trans.). University of Wisconsin Press.

Shengold, L. (1993). *The boy will come to nothing.* Yale University Press.

Stekel, W. (1950). *The autobiography of Wilhelm Stekel.* Liveright.

Wittels, F. (1924). *Sigmund Freud: His personality, his teachings and his school.* Dodd, Mead & Company.

Wittels, F. (1995). *Freud and the child woman: The memoirs of Fritz Wittels.* Yale University Press.

Part II

Chapter 5

Biology and Experience in Freud's Thought

The issues surrounding Freud, fathers, and paternal authority played out not only in his personal dilemmas but in his theories. The other side of the Freud story is how his mostly choosing internal over external reality rather than integrating them caused problems for the adequacy of his psychoanalytic conceptions. This was true in his vacillations over the relationship between biology and experience, the scientific status of psychoanalysis, his theories of Eros and sublimation, the psychological and the progress of civilization, his writings on love, and the divisions within his development of the Oedipus complex over 40 years. Explicating the sufficiency of his views in these areas is the subject of the second part of this book.

As mentioned, Freud's doctrines regularly chose the internal over an integration of human social and psychical realities. Oddly enough, for a period from 1905 to 1913, he renewed his internal dialogue of the 1890s as to which was more important the internal unconscious or other kinds of experiences. Freud by 1915 resolved his uncertainty by again affirming the internal over the external. He did so in a way that resembled his 1897 affirmation of fantasy over other actual events. His vacillations, divisions, and the one-sided ways he internally resolved his dialectic are worth revisiting. They confirm that overall Freud was more partial to choosing psychic over material reality.

During this early 20th-century period, Freud's thinking on the relationship of biology and experience often moves in opposite directions at the same time. Then starting in 1913 and becoming consolidated around 1915, Freud embraces a radical theory that points in one direction rather than several. In both instances, Freud's thought vacillates for a while, and then he makes the characteristic decision to choose the internal over the external. Yet still he makes contradictory statements on biology and experience into the 1930s. This chapter first traces Freud's vacillations, then shows how his theories are dependent on Haeckel and Lamarck's notions of phylogenetic inheritance. Remove the phylogenetic inheritance and the invariability of Freudian phantasies is questionable.

DOI: 10.4324/9781041074717-8

Biology, Bedrock, Complemental Series, and Psychoanalytic Autonomy

His statements on the importance of biology for psychoanalytic understanding from the 1890s until the 1930s not only have fluctuations, but on occasion are actually contradictory. Toward the end of his life in 1937, Freud wrote: "for the psychical field, the biological field does in fact play the part of the underlying bedrock" (Freud, 1964 [1937], SE XXIII, p. 252). Just two years earlier in 1935, Freud had declared: "we must keep psychoanalysis separate from biology" (Freud, 1990 [1935], p. 340). That is one notable reverse. But there is also something additional. Off and on through his career Freud proclaims that psychoanalysis should be independent from other fields. How it is possible to seriously consider the proper relationship of biology and experience while excluding all the research and findings from other academic specialties is beyond me. Still, he proclaims that psychoanalysis should exclude findings from other fields. Listen to Freud.

In 1913, he had written that it is "necessary to hold aloof from biological considerations...so that we may not be misled in our impartial judgment of the psychoanalytic facts before us" (Freud, 1955 [1913], SE XIII, pp. 181–182). For "psycho-analysis must keep itself free from any hypothesis that is alien to it, whether of an anatomical, chemical or physiological kind, and must operate entirely with purely psychological auxiliary ideas" (Freud, 1963 [1916], p. 21). Freud did not want "to subordinate the psychological material to *bio*logical considerations," nor did he want psychoanalysis to be dependent "on philosophy, physiology, or brain anatomy" (McGuire, 1974 [1911], p. 469). Freud says: "We must at all costs remain independent and maintain our equal rights" (Freud, 1965 [1914], p. 171).

Freud insists that the separation of psychoanalysis from other disciplines need not be permanent. Once "we have completed our psychoanalytic work we shall have to find a point of contact with biology" (Freud, 1955 [1913], SE XIII, p. 182). "Ultimately," he writes, "we shall be able to come together with all the parallel sciences" (Freud, 1955 [1914], SE XIII, p. 171). Freud during his lifetime never did make reconciliation in ways the parallel sciences regularly respected.

Again, he is not always consistent. In a 1911 letter, he says: "The question as to which is of greater significance, constitution or experience...can in my opinion only be answered by saying that...not one or the other are decisive" (Freud, 1960 [1911], SE XII, p. 284). Twenty years later, Freud confesses: "we are not as yet able to distinguish...between what is rigidly fixed by biological laws and what is open to movement and change under the influence of accidental experience" (Freud, 1961 [1931], SE XXI, p. 242). There are occasions where Freud stresses the priority of actual experiences. "In our analytic work we concentrate more on the accidental influences than on the constitutional factors" (Freud, 1960 [1911], p. 284). In 1913, Freud declares that "psychoanalysis has fully demonstrated the part played by social conditions...in the causation of neurosis" (Freud, 1955 [1913], SE XIII,

p. 188). Then, at other times, Freud sees a balance between inherited and acquired characteristics. The "relation between the" constitutional and accidental factors

> is a co-operative and not a mutually exclusive one. The constitutional factor must await experiences before it can make itself felt; the accidental factor must have a constitutional basis in order to come into operation. To cover the majority of cases, we can picture what has been described as a 'complemental series,' in which the diminishing intensity of one factor is balanced by the increasing intensity of the other.
>
> (Freud, 1953 [1905], SE VII, pp. 105–106)

"Disposition and experience," Freud writes, "are...linked up in an indissoluble unity" (Freud, 1957 [1914], SE XIV, p. 18). We do not know which has priority, then on occasion he says psychoanalysis focuses on accidental experience, and then there is a unity. He also gives prominence to biology.

> In spite of all our efforts to prevent biological terminology and considerations from dominating psychoanalytic work, we cannot avoid using them even in our descriptions of the phenomena that we study. We cannot help regarding the term 'instinct' as a concept on the frontier between the spheres of psychology and biology.
>
> (Freud, 1955 [1913], SE XIII, p. 182)

It is not likely that these diverging statements can be integrated into a whole.

Over time, Freud abandons his inconsistencies and affirms a doctrine in which biology supersedes accidental experience. Beginning in 1911 but then increasing from 1913 on Freud fully embraces and extensively utilizes the biological concepts of the phylogenetic inheritance and recapitulation. In these notions, the individual absorbs and internalizes the experiences of the past. In the phylogenetic inheritance, the imagination reorders experience to have it fit into an ancient inherited mental pattern. Biologist Stephen Jay Gould writes that "Freud often argued that the general libidinal development of individuals recapitulates a sequence of stages in the history of civilization." For "Freud's general theory of neuroses and psychoanalysis relies" on "mental recapitulation" (Gould, 1977, pp. 159, 157). As well, Frank Sulloway recognizes, "phylogeny was Freud's final answer to many of the difficulties that threatened to undermine his most basic psychoanalytic claims" (Sulloway, 1992, p. 388). Though he may insist on the rigid theoretical separation of biology and his newly developed discipline, in practice Freudian psychoanalytic theory from 1913 on rests on a biological base that places inheritance above current experience.

With all his going back and forth, in Freud's writings, what eventually prevails is a return to the biological bedrock of the human condition. We are born immature and need others to care for us; we also go through a variety of biologically programmed developmental stages. Biological forces lead to psychological developments.

Though at times Freud seems to embrace the notion of a complemental series and the importance of the social, his actual expositions focus much more on the internal than the mix of the psychic and social. As well, these statements about experience being crucial are more frequent before 1914. From then on until his death he most characteristically leaned toward claim that the imagination reorders experience.

The Phylogenetic Inheritance and the Psychoanalytic Psyche

Freud explains how: the "*constitutional* factor in the individual" derives from what is "innately present in him at his birth, elements with a phylogenetic origin" (Freud, 1964 [1939], SE XXIII, p. 98). On the one hand, in 1915, Freud asserts that "the phylogenetic disposition…should find no contradiction if the individual adds new dispositions from his own experience to his inherited disposition" (Freud, 1987 [1915], p. 10). On the other hand, in 1918 Freud, in describing the Wolf Man, says "the boy…fit himself into a phylogenetic pattern…although his personal experiences may not have agreed with it" (Freud, 1955 [1918], SE XVII, p.86). For the "phylogenetic foundation has…the upper hand over personal accidental experience" (Freud, 1964 [1940], SE XXIII, p. 45). These "phylogenetically inherited schema…are concerned with the business of 'placing' the impressions derived from actual experience….Wherever experiences fail to fit in with the hereditary schema, they become remodeled in the imagination" (Freud, 1955 [1918], SE XVII, p. 119). Freud traces the phylogenetic inheritance back to what he calls the pre-history of human civilization. "The Oedipus complex…is, in fact, the best known member of the class" (Freud, 1955 [1918], SE XVII, p. 119).

Freud's particular conception of the phylogenetically inherited schema clearly fits experience into a pre-determined pattern. It allows Freud to focus on the intrapsychic determinants more than on the complemental series. Emphasizing phylogeny allows Freud to give a foundation for what takes place in the unconscious. The forms human phantasies take can be seen as a product of our inheritance. The biologically derived human imagination remodels experience to fit its own needs. As well, the priority given to phylogeny allows Freud to turn away from the complications of weaving together nature and nurture, the intra and inter psychic. Despite his contradictory utterances and his frequent vacillations, there are many elements in Freud's theories, as Sulloway observes, that are ultimately dependent upon the concept of the phylogenetic inheritance. Taking a critical look at Freud's use of phylogeny is crucial for understanding Freudian psychoanalytic theory.

The Phylogenetic Inheritance

The psychoanalyst father's notion of a phylogenetic inheritance is derived from the work of Darwin, Lamarck, Haeckel, Atkinson, and Robertson Smith. Phylogeny is the evolutionary development of a species. To Freud, "each individual somehow recapitulates in an abbreviated form the entire development of the human race" (Freud, 1963 [1915–1916], SE XV, p. 199). He believes that

> *primal phantasies*...are a phylogenetic endowment. In them the individual reaches beyond his own experience into primeval experience at points where his own experience has been too rudimentary. It seems to me quite possible that all the things that are told to us to-day in analysis as phantasy...were once real occurrences in the primeval times of the human family.
>
> (Freud, 1963 [1916–1917], SE XVI, p. 371)

Freud traces the origin of primal phantasy back to events in what he calls the "pre-history" of the human race. What Freud proceeds to do is use his just so *Totem and Taboo* tale into the phylogenetic inheritance that impacts all humans. This means that incestuous desires for the mother and rebellion and acquiescence to fathers are written into the heart of our mental apparatus. No matter what our experience may be within our lives, the phylogenetic inheritance directs us to imagine a mother and father. To Freud, the past is not only prologue but determining.

In *Totem and Taboo* he incorporates the fathers, band of brothers and sexually desirable females of our pre-history into every succeeding generation. Given how Freud applies what he develops in this 1913 work, it deserves explication. Following Darwin and Atkinson, Freud postulates a primal horde. "Darwin," Freud writes, "deduced from the habits of the higher apes that men, too, originally lived in comparatively small groups or hordes within which the jealousy of the oldest and strongest male prevented sexual promiscuity" (Freud, 1955 [1913], SE XIII, p. 125). The dominant male in "Darwin's primal horde....is a violent and jealous father who keeps all the females for himself and drives away his sons as they grow up" (Freud, 1955 [1913], SE XIII, p. 141). This father, Freud asserts, also "compelled all his sons to be abstinent" (Freud, 1955 [1921], SE XVIII, p. 92).

After being expelled from their family some of the sons "might...establish a similar horde, in which the same prohibition upon sexual intercourse would rule owing to the leader's jealousy" (Freud, 1955 [1913], SE XIII, p. 126). Not every son was able to establish his own hordes; many lived together as a band of brothers. According to Freud,

> One day the brothers who had been driven out came together, killed and devoured their father and so made an end of the patriarchal horde. United, they had the courage to do and succeeded in doing what would have been impossible for them individually.
>
> (Freud, 1955 [1913], SE XIII, p. 141)

With the father murdered, this might have been seen as the best of all possible worlds, both men and women were free to join together sexually without any controlling authority. But parricide was not psychologically and sexually liberating. For after their father's violent death,

> the tumultuous mob of brothers were filled with...contradictory feelings....They hated their father...but they loved and admired him too. After they had got rid of him...the affection which had all this time been pushed under was bound to make itself felt. It did so in the form of remorse. A sense of guilt made its appearance, which in this instance coincided with the remorse felt by the whole group.
>
> (Freud, 1955 [1913], SE XIII, p. 143)

The emancipated brothers collectively decided to prohibit killing of the father and abandoned their sexual claims on the newly freed females. Parricide and incest were forbidden. These collective decisions are, to Freud, "the first social ties, the basic moral restrictions" (Freud, 1955 [1919], SE XVII, p. 262). They are Freud's version of the social contract. For "parricide and incest with the mother are the two great human crimes, the only ones which...are pursued and abhorred in primitive communities" (Freud, 1957 [1916], SE XIV, p. 333).

Yet this attempt at renunciation by the band of brothers was not completely successful. To Freud, "the son's sense of guilt and the son's rebelliousness...never became extinct" (Freud, 1955 [1913], SE XIII, p. 152). It is re-enacted by each male child in the Oedipus complex. To Freud, there is a "tragic guilt" that stems from "rebellion against...authority" (Freud, 1955 [1913], SE XIII, p. 156). Freud, as mentioned, concludes "that the problems of social psychology...prove soluble on the basis of one single concrete point-man's relation to his father" (Freud, 1955 [1913], SE XIII, p. 157).

The origins of this primal rebellion, according to Freud, are in the days before recorded history. To this day, unconscious memory traces from the distant past remain. Freud maintains that "what may be operative in an individual's psychic life may include not only what he has experienced himself but also things that were innately present in him at his birth, elements with a phylogenetic origin" (Freud, 1964 [1939], SE XXIII, p. 98). He writes:

> it is a plausible hypothesis to suppose that a primeval and prehistoric demand has at last become part of the organized and inherited endowment of mankind. A child who produces instinctual repressions spontaneously is thus merely repeating a part of the history of civilization. What is today an act of internal restraint was once an external one.
>
> (Freud, 1955 [1913], SE XIII, pp. 188–189)

How then did the external restraints of humankind's pre-history become part of our phylogenetic inheritance? They do so, Freud says, through "a memory trace" that becomes part of "the archaic heritage if the event was important enough, or repeated often enough, or both. In the case of parricide both conditions are fulfilled" (Freud, 1964 [1939], SE XXIII, p. 101). To Freud, these events "occurred to all primitive men...it covered thousands of years and was repeated countless times" (Freud, 1964 [1939], SE XXIII, p. 81).

How does Freud know this? How can something like the primal horde hypothesis possibly be verified? Freud admits that "the transformation of the paternal horde into a community of brothers....is only a hypothesis....a 'Just-So Story,'... but I think it creditable to such a hypothesis if it proves able to bring coherence and understanding into more and more new regions" (Freud, 1955 [1921], SE XVIII, p. 69). He admits that his hypothesis about the prehistoric human family and its fate is in certain respects "founded upon the observations of Robertson Smith" (Freud, 1955 [1919], SE XVII, p. 262). In *Moses and Monotheism*, Freud recognizes that "more recent ethnologists have unanimously rejected Robertson Smith's hypothesis" (Freud, 1964 [1939], SE XXIII, p. 131). How does Freud respond to the abandonment of Smith's theory by the scholars in the field? "I have not been convinced...of Robertson Smith's errors," he declares, "....I am not an ethnologist but a psycho-analyst. I had a right to take out of ethnological literature what I might need for the work of analysis" (Freud, 1964 [1939], SE XXIII, p. 131). In other words, psychoanalysis needs an ethnological foundation, even if this particular foundation was discredited by the experts in ethnology.

As well, Freud adhered to the notions of Lamarck that traits acquired through the experience of one individual can be passed on to descendants. He was cognizant that Lamarck's ideas were not acceptable to scientists. "My position...is made more difficult by the present attitude of biological science, which refuses to hear of the inheritance of acquired characteristics by succeeding generations....I cannot do without this factor in biological evolution" (Freud, 1964 [1939], SE XXIII, p. 100). As he told Joseph Wortis: "Of course, if one didn't believe in inheritance, there would be a great deal we could not explain" (Wortis, 1940, p. 847). Freud pinpoints his own dilemma. He cannot have a coherent psychoanalytic theory without turning to claims that are empirically untenable, and rejected by science.

Freud turned to concepts that had inheritance overriding experience for good reasons. Without the phylogenetic inheritance, Freud's theories would have significant explanatory gaps. Phylogeny provided a foundation for primal phantasies. Without the phylogenetic inheritance, psychoanalysis would need another theory of how the mind works to explain how the imagination structures experience. As Freud favors the internal over the external, phylogeny gives him a justification for his frequent underplaying of actual experiences. Psychoanalysis, as Freud conceived it, is quite dependent on the discredited phylogenetic inheritance to explain how the unconscious reorders experience.

How a Doctrine of Biological Inheritance Enhances Psychoanalytic Universals

There are at least three ways that the phylogenetic inheritance eliminated certain dilemmas otherwise present. First, the foundation of the Oedipus complex is in the child choosing the nourishing figure as the first object choice. Freud proposes that because of our inheritance the imagination ensures that this is the mother, whether or not the child ever "enjoyed the tenderness of a mother's care" (Freud, 1964 [1940], SE XXIII, p. 188). Should a baby be breast fed by a wet nurse, in the child's imagination the other woman who gives the child her breast "is as a rule merged into the mother" (Freud, 1964 [1933], SE XXII, p.122). Without the phylogenetic base, the first object choice could be a Nannie or wet nurse, or there could be multiple initial object choices rather than one.

In 18th-century France, infants were often sent from Paris to the country to be raised by a wet nurse for a few years and then sent back to the capital to be raised by their mother, if they survived (Coles, 2015). There are also multiple instances where children raised from birth in orphanages have no reliable nurturers and do not form attachments with any human (Nelson et al., 2014). These facts raise questions about there being a mother present to whom the child becomes attached and develops sexual desire for her. Without the phylogenetic base, Freud would need to show how these multiple instances where children did not have a single reliable female caregiver would develop the mother as object choice.

Second, without phylogeny, Freud has difficulty explaining the universality of the father as a rival. Not all families have fathers or other males present, and in some families, like Freud's own, he saw the older brother as a more important rival than the fully present father. Identification with the father is a prerequisite for the resolution of the Oedipus complex. If a father or other male is not there to stand between the child and the mother, and the biological imagination does not create a father image for the child, then how can the Oedipus complex develop?

Third, the castration complex is another crucial component of Freud's Oedipal theory. The threats of castration, Freud has said, usually originate with the mother, but the phylogenetic imagination re-frames the threats as coming from the father, because, as Freud says, "in man's pre-history it was unquestionably the father who practised castration as a punishment" (Freud, 1955 [1918], SE XVII, p. 86). Take away the reliance on the ancient history of the human race, and it would be from women that most male children would usually fear losing their penis. In Freud's Oedipal theory, it is fear of the father castrating the child that causes the boy to abandon the mother as a love-object, identify with the father, develop a super-ego, and move into the latency period. Remove the part of the imagination that makes the father the potential castrator and the male Oedipus complex cannot proceed universally as Freud envisioned. As he often gave less close attention to the diversity of external influences on the child, the theory of phylogenetic inheritance enabled him to evade the complexity and diversity of actual experience in relation to the Oedipus complex.

Without the phylogenetic inheritance to fall back on, Freud's theories face significant challenges. Since psychoanalysis, according to Freud, is the science of the unconscious, having gaps in how the unconscious functions creates problems for his whole theoretical edifice. In particular, primal phantasies are a crucial component of the Freudian unconscious. Remove the phylogenetic origin of phantasy and where phantasy originates and how uniform or diverse phantasies are becomes problematic. Given the multiplicity of options, without the phylogenetic inheritance there is a big hole in the center of the psychoanalytic theory of the unconscious.

Therein lies the rub for Freudian psychoanalysis; he needs a reliable method of reproducing its findings. The phylogenetic inheritance provides psychoanalysis with such an underlying bedrock, even if it was in Freud's day and still remains scientifically untenable. There is, of course, another irony here. Freud's following his own ideas and carrying them through enabled him to go beyond the science of his day to create the new domain of psychoanalysis. Like much, his boldness is a double-edged sword, reflecting innovations and theoretical gaps. On the relationship of biology and experience, too often it was easier for him to turn to phylogeny than confront the gaps arising from his doctrines. His turning to recapitulation and the phylogenetic inheritance allowed him to reinstate with a vengeance his 1897 separating the internal from the external. To his theoretical detriment, the great irony of Freud's legacy is that he opened up so many new paths to human self-understanding and yet he so often shied away from confronting the complexities that actual experience brought to his grand theories.

References

Coles, P. (2015). *The shadow of the second mother*. Routledge.

Freud, S. (1953). *Three essays on the theory of sexuality, The standard edition of the complete psychological works, Vol. VII* (J. Strachey Ed. and Trans.). The Hogarth Press, pp. 125–245 (Original work published 1905).

Freud, S. (1955). The claims of psycho-analysis to scientific interest. *The standard edition of the complete psychological works, Vol. XIII* (J. Strachey Ed. and Trans.). The Hogarth Press, pp. 165–190 (Original work published 1913).

Freud, S. (1955). *Totem and Taboo, The standard edition of the complete psychological works, Vol. XIII* (J. Strachey Ed. and Trans.). The Hogarth Press, pp. 1–162 (Original work published 1913).

Freud, S. (1955). From the history of an infantile neurosis. *The standard edition of the complete psychological works, Vol. XVII* (J. Strachey Ed. and Trans.). The Hogarth Press, pp. 3–123 (Original work published 1918).

Freud, S. (1955). Preface to Reik's *Ritual: Psycho-analytic Studies, The standard edition of the complete psychological works, Vol. XVII* (J. Strachey Ed. and Trans.). The Hogarth Press, pp. 257–263 (Original work published 1919).

Freud, S. (1955). *Group psychology and the analysis of the ego, The standard edition of the complete psychological works, Vol. XVIII* (J. Strachey Ed. and Trans.). The Hogarth Press, pp. 67–143 (Original work published 1921).

Freud, S. (1957). *On the history of the Psychoanalytic movement, The standard edition of the complete psychological works, Vol. XIV* (J. Strachey Ed. and Trans.). The Hogarth Press, pp. 3–66 (Original work published 1914).

Freud, S. (1957). Some character-types met with in Psychoanalytic work. *The standard edition of the complete psychological works, Vol. XIV* (J. Strachey Ed. and Trans.). The Hogarth Press, pp. 309–333 (Original work published 1916).

Freud, S. (1960). Letter to Else Voigtlander, October 1, 1911, *Letters of Sigmund Freud* (E. Freud Ed.). Basic Books, p. 284.

Freud, S. (1961). Female sexuality. *The standard edition of the complete psychological works, Vol. XXI* (J. Strachey Ed. and Trans.). The Hogarth Press, pp. 223–243 (Original work published 1931).

Freud, S. (1963). *Introductory lecture on psycho-analysis, parts I and II, The standard edition of the complete psychological works, Vol. XV* (J. Strachey Ed. and Trans.). The Hogarth Press (Original work published 1915–1916).

Freud, S. (1964). *New introductory lectures on psycho-analysis. The standard edition of the complete psychological work Vol. XXII* (J. Strachey Ed. and Trans.). The Hogarth Press, pp. 5–157 (Original work published 1933).

Freud, S. (1964). Analysis terminal and interminable. *The standard edition of the complete psychological work Vol. XXIII* (J. Strachey Ed. and Trans.). The Hogarth Press, pp. 211–253 (Original work published 1937).

Freud, S. (1964). *Moses and monotheism, The standard edition of the complete psychological work Vol. XXIII* (J. Strachey Ed. and Trans.). The Hogarth Press, pp. 3–137 (Original work published 1939).

Freud, S. (1964). *An Outline of psycho-analysis, The standard edition of the complete psychological works, Vol. XXIII* (J. Strachey Ed. and Trans.). The Hogarth Press, pp. 141–207 (Original work published 1940).

Freud, S. (1965). *A Psycho-analytic dialogue: The Letters of Sigmund Freud and Karl Abraham, 1907–1926* (H. Abraham and E. Freud Ed.; B. Marsh and H. Abraham Trans.). Basic Books (Original work written 1914).

Freud, S. (1987). *A phylogenetic fantasy: Overview of the transference neuroses* (I. Grubrich-Simitis Ed.; A. Hoffer and P. Hoffer Trans.). Harvard University Press.

Freud, S. (1990). Letter to Carl Mueller-Braunschweig, July 21, 1935, *Freud on Women* (E. Young-Bruehl Ed.). W. W. Norton & Company, p. 340.

Gould, S. (1977). *Ontogeny and phylogeny.* Harvard University Press.

McGuire, W. (1974). *The Freud/Jung letters: The correspondence between Sigmund Freud and C. G. Jung* (W. McGuire Ed.). Princeton University Press.

Nelson, C., Fox, N., and Zeanah, C. (2014). *Romania's abandoned children: Deprivation, brain development, and the struggle for recovery.* Harvard University Press.

Sulloway, F. (1992). *Freud, biologist of the mind.* Harvard University Press.

Wortis, J. (1940). Fragments of a Freudian analysis. *Orthopsychiatry*, Volume X, pp. 843–849.

Chapter 6

Freud, Psychoanalysis, and Science

Freud acknowledging that he employed theories rejected by scholars as unscientific leads to a connected subject matter. Freud on numerous occasions described psychoanalysis as the science of the unconscious. It is worth pausing the explication of the external and internal in Freud to examine his claims about his specialty being empirically sound.

The most vehement criticisms of Freud's thoughts are connected to his allegedly deviating from scientific standards. There is an irony here. Sigmund Freud himself believed he had founded a new science with great significance. To him, his discoveries, like those of Copernicus and Darwin, wounded human self-love. The "psychological research of the present time…seeks to prove to the ego that it is not even master in its own house, but must content itself with scanty information of what is going on unconsciously in its mind" (Freud, 1963 [1916], SE XVI, p. 285). For Freud, psychoanalysis is not "a subsidiary science in the field of psychopathology," but "the foundation for a new and deeper science of the mind which would be equally indispensable for the understanding of the normal. Its postulates and findings could be carried over…into spheres of universal interest" (Freud, 1959 [1925], SE XX, p. 47). Psychoanalysis, this new and deeper field, is "the science of unconscious mental processes" (Freud, 1959 [1925], SE XX, p. 70).

Not everyone had as high opinion of Freud's creation as he did. Some of his critics have insisted that his formulations are more speculation than science. This skepticism of the scientific credibility of Freud's claims is the demon that has haunted psychoanalysis. Outside and inside the field observers criticize Freud's methods and doctrines. This chapter examines these controversies over science.

There are judgments of Freud's theories that are quite harsh. Harvard philosopher Donald C. Williams declares that "psychoanalysis is…much more like alchemy, for example, than chemistry" in that it has a "dearth of statistical test and crucial experiment and indeed of any clear logical nexus between principles and observation" (Williams, 1959, p. 172). Chemist and philosopher Michael Polanyi sees the "Freudian system" as "a largely conjectural and rather vague doctrine" (Polanyi, 1958, p. 139). Still another philosopher, Karl Popper, maintains that Freud's theories are "simply non-testable, irrefutable. There was no conceivable human behavior which could contradict them" (Popper, 1962, p. 37).

DOI: 10.4324/9781041074717-9

In 1971, philosopher Alasdair MacIntyre wrote that psychoanalytic theory "is certainly no better confirmed-and perhaps not as well confirmed-as witchcraft and astrology" (MacIntyre, 1971, p. 8). Four years later, distinguished biologist P. B. Medawar declared that "doctrinaire psychoanalytic theory is the most stupendous intellectual confidence trick of the twentieth century...a vast structure of radically unsound design and with no posterity" (Medawar, 1975, p. 17). Philosopher Patricia Kitcher writes that psychoanalysis "is widely regarded as the paradigm of bad science, a theory so obviously false that its proponents must be deluded or devious or perhaps both" (Kitcher, 1992, p. 153).

Over time, some psychoanalysts expressed concerns about the scientific credibility of their field. Analytic stalwart Martin Bergmann writes, "Disagreements between psychoanalytic schools were not those encountered in the natural sciences, which further experiments eventually resolve, but more closely resembled religious and philosophical disputes, which cannot be resolved by rational means" (Bergmann, 2004, p. 2). Former President of the International Psychoanalytical Association, Robert Wallerstein, writes, "psychoanalytic clinicians can construct differing but equally plausible and compelling formulations of psychoanalytic case material, yet at the same time have no systematic method for establishing the truth claims of any of the alternatives" (Wallerstein, 1993, p. 97).

Analyst Dale Boesky concurs: psychoanalysis as a discipline is "unable to scientifically prove that any theory is better or worse than any other about anything at all." It also has "no consensually accepted methodology to guide us in understanding how the analyst infers meanings from the raw data of the patient's communication" (Boesky, 2008, pp. 6, 11, 3). Yale's Marshall Edelson said that psychoanalysis has an "inability to quantify variables." It needs to show "causal links" between "unconscious fantasies" and "observable phenomena." The problem is these "causal links...are often complex if not downright torturous" (Edelson, 1988, p. 96).

Freud on Science and Psychoanalysis

Freud, however, had his own perspectives on science and psychoanalysis. In his 1932 exchange with Albert Einstein, Freud writes to the eminent physicist, "It may perhaps seem to you as though our theories are a kind of mythology....But does not every science come in the end to a kind of mythology like this? Cannot the same be said to-day of your own Physics" (Freud, 1964 [1932], SE XXII, p. 211).

Earlier in 1932, Freud had written more extensively on the relationship of science to psychoanalysis. He started then by saying that a *Weltanschauung* "is an intellectual construction which solves all the problems of our existence on the basis of one overriding hypothesis" (Freud, 1964 [1932–1933], SE XXII, p, 158). Psychoanalysis, he asserts, does not need a world view "of its own....it is part of science, and can adhere to the scientific *Weltanschauung*" (Freud, 1964 [1932–1933], SE XXII, p. 181). The psychoanalytic "contribution to science lies precisely in having extended research to the mental field" (Freud, 1964 [1932–1933], SE XXII, p. 159).

To him, what was the science to which his psychoanalysis was a part? Science, Freud declares, is a "sphere of knowledge" that contains "carefully scrutinized observations." He writes that it "is content to investigate and establish facts." How does science do this? It does so by providing "itself with new perceptions...and it isolates the determinants of these new experiences in experiments." The goal is to "arrive at correspondence with reality." Science works with "conjectures" and "hypothesis" which "we withdraw if they are not confirmed" (Freud, 1964 [1932–1933], SE XXII, pp. 160, 159, 162, 170, 174).

When the question becomes who carefully scrutinizes the observations and experiments, ascertains what are facts, and what hypothesis are confirmed and what rejected, Freud has stipulations. Despite his declared allegiance to science, Freud often, but not always, takes the stance that he is a revolutionary outsider battling the conservative establishment. He declared that "conflict with official science" was the "destiny" of psychoanalysis (Freud, 1955 [1913], SE XIII, p. 169).

Still, Freud does attempt to explain how the psychoanalytic process can be scientific.

> We have discovered technical methods of filling up the gaps in the phenomena of our consciousness, and we make use of those methods just as the physicist makes use of experiment. In this manner we deduce a number of processes which are in themselves 'unknowable' and insert them among the processes of which we are conscious. And if, for instance, we say: 'At this point an unconscious memory intervened,' what this means is: 'At this point something occurred of which we are totally unable to form a conception, but which, if it had entered our consciousness, could only have been described in such and such a way.
>
> (Freud, 1964 [1940], SE XXIII, pp. 196–197)

Freud has moved from observables to deducing processes that are unknowable and asserting that these unknowables can only be described in a particular way. "The relative certainty of our psychical science," Freud writes, "is based on the binding force of...inferences....our technique holds its ground against any criticism" (Freud 1964 [1940], SE XXIII, p. 159).

Can Freud show how these relatively certain and bold descriptions can withstand rigorous evaluation? Despite this declaration of confidence, Freud becomes choosy about how his theories can be examined. In 1934, in writing to American academic psychologist Saul Rosensweig Freud asserts that "the wealth of dependable observations" makes psychoanalysis "independent of experimental verification" (Gay, 1988, p. 523). This 1934 assertion is not consistent with his affirming two years earlier that thorough testing of empirical claims through verifiable experiments was integral to science. Freud's assertion is contrary to that principle. Instead, Freud claims that his technical methodology provides a wealth of dependable information and further examination is unnecessary.

But later he admits that there is "the lack of agreement among analysts." He attributed it to problems with training, the newness of the discipline, and that the subject matter of psychoanalysis "unlike physics," does not always "arouse a cool scientific interest" (Freud, 1964 [1940], SE XXIII, p. 197). As often happens, Freud is moving in divergent directions. At first, he asserts there are relatively certain dependable observations but then acknowledges that analysts disagree, and so the claims are neither dependable nor certain.

To remedy these epistemological problems, psychoanalysis would need to evolve so that observations could be tested by reliable observers. To achieve that goal Freud would have had to propose replicable methods for evaluating the contradictory claims of different analysts. Yet, from 1900 on Freud does not proceed to set up procedures and standards by which the lack of agreement can be adjudicated, and reliable and replicable conclusions can occur. He abandons the scientific standards he previously asserted were integral to scientific inquiries.

Furthermore, the disagreement among analysts has not abated. No field wide consensus has developed on how to evaluate different claims and interpretations. His insistence that the psychoanalytic process leads to one agreed upon conclusion remains a problem as the persistence of disagreement among the various psychoanalytic factions undercuts the claim of a consensus. His explication of the scientific claims of his field were contradicted by his own admissions.

In addition, as previously discussed, Freud adhered to something called the phylogenetic inheritance, which claims that prior experience of the species can override individual experience in a person's psyche. To repeat, he knew the ethnologists of his day thought this notion was not scientific. His response, "I am not an ethnologist but a psycho-analyst. I had a right to take out of ethnological literature what I might need for the work of analysis" (Freud 1964 [1939], SE XXIII, p. 131). He has previously admitted that Lamarck too is rejected by science, but he still adheres to it.

The founder of psychoanalysis had previously said when evidence does not confirm hypothesis then scientists abandoned them. He also had done the same when declaring that he did not need verification from psychological experiments. It should be remembered that Freud often vowed to keep psychoanalysis separate from biology and other scientific endeavors to maintain the field's independence. It is easier to find examples of Freud's deviance from scientific standards of verifying research than of his showing how psychoanalysis met scientific criteria for reliability.

Clearly, Freud did not make the effort to work out the principles and methods that could have his field fit comfortably into the scientific *Weltanschauung*. Still, he is onto something that the study of the unconscious can open up new areas for scientific understanding. But because he did not make the effort after 1900 to pass scientific muster, Freud has opened the way for both dedicated psychoanalysts and Freud bashers to criticize the status of psychoanalysis as a legitimate science.

Psychiatrist and historian of psychoanalysis, George Makari, maintains that early on Freud abandoned science for dogmatism. Dr Makari believes he has pinpointed when Freud crossed the line from investigator to doctrinaire theorist. At the Nuremberg psychoanalytic conference in 1910, Freud called for "standardization" and "uniformity." The problem was that "invariance" runs "counter to the requirements of scientific research, which called for freedom of inquiry" (Makari, 2008, pp. 240–241). To Makari, "Freud's Achilles heel" was that the libido theory "seemed to flout the rules of empiricism and scientific epistemology" (Makari, 2008, p. 263). And that that "post-Nuremberg" findings "that contradicted the theory were not acceptable." Gone were the days when Freud sought to construct "a psychology of the inner life that conformed with science" (Makari, 2008, p. 296). That Freud's brain-child diverges from scientific principles is the elephant in the psychoanalytic room.

He protected his psychoanalysis from the same empirical standards he proclaimed were indispensable in science. On occasion, when research rejected doctrines, in the name of his own freedom, he chose doctrine over evidence. Sigmund Freud had less allegiance to science than to his own intellectual liberty.

The following detailed account of scientific practice by physician James C. Zimring helps illuminate what was missing from psychoanalysis under Freud.

Zimring:

> challenging ideas with deep skepticism is not just a cultural norm in the sciences, but not engaging in such activities is a 'no-'no.' I have many scientific colleagues that I consider to be close friends, and what we do at our annual meetings is go up to the microphone and try to discredit each other's ideas in a public forum. This is not bad manners – this is what we are supposed to do. It is woven into the fabric of modern science to scrutinize both one's own observations and the claims of others by processes specifically designed to compensate for the sources of human observational error.
>
> (Zimring, 2019, p. 274)

In contrast, Freud was not often receptive to other means of evaluating psychoanalysis, nor to rigorous empirical investigations being turned on his own doctrines. He was often one-sided. It is not surprising then that when it came to embracing outside examination that Freud vehemently shied away from endorsing that. As he reportedly said to Jung when asked to share more details about his dreams, Freud deferred. Then Jung reports Freud said "I cannot risk my authority" (Clark, 1980, p. 265).

Whether or not Jung's account is accurate, this claim about authority was not uncommon for Freud, who worried about heresy. Despite this, there is the paradox that Freud was one of the great theoretical innovators in Western history. Unfortunately, the judgment of Freudian psychoanalysis as outside of science is too often confirmed. This is unfortunate as psychoanalysis certainly covers subject matter within the domains of scientific inquiry. Freud's frequently choosing doctrine over rigorous testing of his claims has stained his credibility with scientists and philosophers.

To sum up, there were problems with Freud's claims of some certainty and ability to withstand critiques. First, he was not receptive to all means of testing psychoanalysis, including when approached by an American empirical psychologist. Second, the findings within his field were not as certain and dependable as he asserted. Third, Freud adopted doctrines that had been already tested and rejected by experts. They were neither dependable nor certain. Critically read, Freud's own declarations undermine his confident claims to relative certainty and scientific confirmation of his doctrines.

Science in Post-Freudian Psychoanalysis

There have been many advances in the natural and social sciences since Freud died in 1939. This scholarship includes findings about the unconscious, consciousness, the brain/mind, the Oedipus complex, the family, biological endowments, sexuality, developmental stages, attachment, dreams, fantasy, creativity, higher mental processes, the self, interpersonal dynamics, narcissism, and more. As well, since Freud's day a number of respected psychoanalysts have sought various means of reconciling psychoanalytic doctrines by conducting research that meets scientific standards. These include Louis Sander, Ed Tronick, Daniel Stern, Beatrice Beeby, Mark Solms, Frank Lachman, among others. There is no research I know of that indicates how far these important findings have become integrated into training in psychoanalytic institutes.

One of these persons, Mark Solms is the Chair of Neuropsychology at the University of Cape Town. Solms writes about what he concludes is an error by Freud. "The mistake in Freud's theoretical model…is a conflation of what he called the 'id' with what he called the 'system unconscious.'" The "part of the brain" that Freud says is the id is not unconscious as Freud stated but "is conscious." Also, what Freud says was part of the conscious ego "is now thought to be intrinsically unconscious." It "turns out that consciousness *is* lodged in the inmost interior of the brain" and "does not stream in through the senses." What "Freud assigned to the id…are all conscious" (Solms, 2017, pp. 90–91). Solms concludes that it is "clear how much psychoanalysis has to gain from incorporating the findings of other disciplines" (Solms, 2017, p. 96).

UCLA neuroscientist Allan Schore would concur. In his 2019 *The Development of the Unconscious Mind,* he directly addresses the Freudian conception of the unconscious. Dr Schore says that newer knowledge in "neuroscience and neuropsychoanalysis" leads to "a major alteration in Freud's conceptualization of a 'dynamic unconscious.'" For "psychoanalytic theory is now being transformed from a theory of the unconscious mind into a theory of brain/mind/body." What Freud said about the dynamic unconscious can now be described as "a hierarchical, self-organizing implicit-procedural regulatory system that is located in the 'emotional' right brain." The unconscious, Schore claims, is not only about "the repressed," but as well is about "defensively dissociated traumatic emotional memories" (Schore, 2019, pp. 21–22).

As does Solms and Schore, Adelphi clinical psychologists Joel Weinberger and Valentina Stoycheva discuss the Freudian unconscious in their 2019

The Unconscious: Theory, Research, and Clinical Implications. They frame their explication in the well-known divide between the empirical approach of academic psychology and the clinical approach of psychoanalysis. They point out that psychoanalysts generally did not "offer empirical data in support of their conceptions." This "lack of empirical emphasis" along with its "separation from the academy weakened its influence" (Weinberger and Stoycheva, 2020, p. 3). The authors note that in psychoanalysis the unconscious was central in the 20th century, but it is only in the 21st century that the study of the unconscious among psychologists, neuroscientists, and cognitive scientists has flourished (2020, p. 7). Freud and other analysts offer much, they say, but need to face rigorous empirical evaluation to be useful.

It is not clear what percentage of analysts incorporate these neuroscience findings in their analytic practice. Psychoanalyst David Lotto is concerned that the field may remain intellectually isolated. He sees the "danger" for psychoanalysis is "becoming insular and isolated" by "listening only to those who are…sympathetic with a psychoanalytic view of the world" (Lotto, 2017, p. 12). The concerns that Bergman had about psychoanalysis being more like religion than science, and that Wallerstein and Boesky had about there being no field wide accepted ways of testing psychoanalytic claims remain. The psychoanalytic movement survives, flourishes, and continues to have unresolved epistemological dilemmas.

There is reason to both pay attention to the insular and more scientific strands within the diverse psychoanalytic fields. Still, there are serious efforts to confront the criticisms of psychoanalysis's scientific status, and do something about them by being more empirical in a scientific sense. After all this time, there are some researchers who are finally confronting the aforementioned demon that has haunted psychoanalysis, its' scientific credibility.

References

Bergmann, M. (2004). *Understanding dissidence and controversy in the history of psychoanalysis.* Other Press.

Boesky, D. (2008). *Psychoanalytic disagreements in context.* Jason Aronson.

Clark, R. (1980). *Freud the man and the cause.* Random House.

Edelson, M. (1988). *Psychoanalysis: A theory in crisis.* University of Chicago Press.

Freud, S. (1955). The claims of psycho-analysis to scientific interest. *The standard edition of the complete psychological works, Vol. XIII* (J. Strachey Ed. and Trans.). The Hogarth Press, pp. 165–190 (Original work published 1913).

Freud, S. (1959). *An autobiographical study. The standard edition of the complete psychological works, Vol. XX* (J. Strachey Ed. and Trans.). The Hogarth Press, pp. 3–74 (Original work published 1925).

Freud, S. (1963). *Introductory lecture on psycho-analysis, parts I and II, The standard edition of the complete psychological works, Vol. XV* (J. Strachey Ed. and Trans.). The Hogarth Press (Original work published 1915–1916).

Freud. S. (1964). Why war?. *The standard edition of the complete psychological works, Vol. XXII* (J. Strachey Ed. and Trans.). The Hogarth Press, pp. 199–215 (Original work published 1932).

Freud, S. (1964). *New introductory lectures on psycho-analysis. The standard edition of the complete psychological works, Vol. XXII* (J. Strachey Ed. and Trans.). The Hogarth Press, pp. 3–182 (Original work published 1933).

Freud, S. (1964). *Moses and monotheism. The standard edition of the complete psychological works, Vol. XXIII* (J. Strachey Ed. and Trans.). The Hogarth Press, pp. 3–137 (Original work published 1939).

Freud, S. (1964). *An outline of psycho-analysis. The standard edition of the complete psychological works, Vol. XXIII* (J. Strachey Ed. and Trans.). The Hogarth Press, pp. 141–207 (Original work published 1940).

Gay, P. (1988). *Freud: A life for our time.* W. W. Norton.

Kitcher, P. (1992). *Freud's dream: A complete interdisciplinary science of the mind.* The MIT Press.

Lotto, D. (2017). On the scientific legitimacy of psychoanalysis: The controversy that won't go away. *Psychoanalytic Discourse*, Volume 4, pp. 5–16.

MacIntyre, A. (1971). *Against the self-images of the age.* University of Notre Dame Press.

Makari, G. (2008). *Revolution in mind: The creation of psychoanalysis.* Harper.

Medawar, P. B. (1975). Victims of psychiatry. *New York Review of Books*, January 23, 1975, p. 17.

Polanyi, M. (1958). *Personal knowledge: Towards a post-critical philosophy.* Harper.

Popper, P. (1962). *Conjectures and refutations.* Basic Books.

Schore, A. (2019). *The development of the unconscious mind.* W. W. Norton & Company.

Solms, M. (2017). What is 'the Unconscious," and where is it located in the brain? A neuropsychoanalytic perspective, *Annals of the New York Academy of Sciences*, Volume 1406, pp. 90–97.

Wallerstein, R. (1993). Psychoanalysis as science: Challenges to the data of psychoanalytic research. *Psychodynamic treatment research: A handbook for clinical practice* (N. Miller, L. Luborsky, J. Barber, and J. Docherty Eds). P. 97. Basic Books.

Weinberger, J. and Stoycheva, V. (2020). *The unconscious: Theory, research and clinical implications.* The Guilford Press.

Williams, D. (1959) Philosophy and psychoanalysis. *Psychoanalysis, scientific method, and philosophy* (S. Hook Ed.). p. 172, New York University Press.

Zimring, J. (2019). *What Science is and how it really works.* Cambridge University Press.

Chapter 7

Civilization's Achievement and Freudian Psychoanalysis

Detailing how Freud ultimately embraced biology over experience while circumventing scientific standards is just part of the Sigmund Freud story. I return now to the relationship in Freud of external, and internal reality. In 1930's *Civilization and Its Discontents*, he comes closer to examining external reality than he normally does. That is not all. Earlier, he also broadened what psychoanalysis tackles. In 1926, Freud proclaimed that "psycho-analysis...developed into a psychology of normal life" (Freud, 1959 [1926], SE XX, pp. 266–267). If normal existence is within the scope of psychoanalysis, then Freud would be obliged to show how the sexualized desires of humans can be drawn to intellectual/emotional/artistical/scientific/technological fields. To see if Freud's doctrines can comprehend these higher mental aims, his notion of the human mental apparatus requires some explication. He has two such theories His initial approach is known as the topographical model, the second as the structural model.

Sigmund Freud and the Unconscious

First, the topographical. In *The Interpretation of Dreams*, Freud refers to four terms concerning our mental apparatus: the conscious, subconscious, preconscious and unconscious. The first two are within the realm of consciousness, which are "those ideas which we observe as active in us, or which we should so observe if we attended to them."

Freud also says that "there are two kinds of unconscious." They are the preconscious and the unconscious. The unconscious, he says, is what is inadmissible to the conscious part of our being. The preconscious "stands like a screen" between the unconscious and consciousness (Freud, 1953 [1900], SE V, pp. 614–615). This preconscious system makes "communication possible between the different ideational contents so that they can influence one another" (Freud, 1957 [1915], SE XIV, p. 188). This entire exposition is known as the topographic model.

Earlier Freud had claimed that "rational and highly complex thought-structures are possible without consciousness playing any part in them" (Freud, 1953 [1900], SE V, p. 616). In the topographic period he does not tackle how highly complex rational thought derives from any of the four parts of our mental structure.

DOI: 10.4324/9781041074717-10

Freud later replaced the topographic model with what has been labeled the structural model. In 1923's *The Ego and the Id,* Freud divides our mental components between the id, ego, and super-ego. The super-ego is a new conceptual innovation. He says that "the 'id'" is that "which behaves as though it were *Ucs*" (Freud, 1961 [1923], SE XIX, p. 23). Most of all, the id, Freud says "is guided by the pleasure principle." It strives "for the satisfaction of the directly sexual trends" (Freud, 1961 [1923], SE XIX, p. 47). The libido also contains aggressiveness (Freud, 1959 [1926], SE XX, p. 106).

Not surprisingly the unconscious can contain opposites, and be unruly. Freud earlier had written that in the unconscious system that there is "no negation, no doubt, no degrees of certainty" for when "instinctual impulses" that are "incompatible become simultaneously active" they do not "cancel each other out" (Freud, 1957 [1915], SE XIV, p. 186).

There is another element in the id, which evolves into something else. He writes, "the ego is that part of the id which has been modified by the direct influence of the external world." The "ego...endeavors to substitute the reality principle for the pleasure principle" (Freud, 1961 [1923], SE XIX, p. 25). This is not an easy task. For in relation to the id, the ego "is like a man on horseback, who has to hold in check the superior strength of the horse." At times, the rider has to let the horse guide its direction. At other times, the ego transforms "the id's will into action as if it were its own" (Freud, 1961 [1923], SE XIX, p. 25). On the one hand, "the ego itself" has an element "which is also unconscious" and "behaves exactly like the repressed." On the other hand, the ego provides "a coherent organization of the mental processes....It is to this ego that consciousness is attached." The Freudian conception of the ego is a divided self; it contains an "antithesis between the coherent ego and the repressed which is split off from it" (Freud, 1961 [1923], XIX, p. 17). The ego's task is both to manage id impulses and adapt to reality.

Then there is the super-ego, which Freud maintains takes "the form of conscience, to exercise the moral censorship." It acts as the enforcer of authority, of its "injunctions and prohibitions" (Freud, 1961 [1923], SE XIX, p. 37). To Freud, the super-ego is "the representative of the internal world, of the id" (Freud, 1961 [1923], SE XIX, p. 36). Internalizing guilt is a large part of the super-ego notion. There is an unconscious element in the super-ego, but one of a different character than the pleasure-seeking id.

Freud slips in another significant element of the unconscious. He says that "subtle and difficult intellectual operations which ordinarily require strenuous reflection can equally be carried out preconsciously and without coming into consciousness....they may occur, for example, during the state of sleep." For instance, upon awakening an individual "knows the solution to a difficult mathematical or other problem with which he had been wrestling with the day before." As well, "mental activities" that are "extremely high" can be "unconscious" and "produce effects of the greatest importance" (Freud, 1961 [1923], SE XIX, pp. 26–27). These subconscious creative processes are not part of the id, ego, or super-ego as Freud describes them. His account of subconscious creativity is tantalizing, yet not integrated into his tri-part theory. Freud brings in an element of the ego that might help us understand how the human mind can undertake such strenuous intellection activity. It is called the reality principle.

The Reality Principle

When Freud writes about the reality principle, he is not addressing the cosmos, or the life of the over eight million earthly species, but reality for *Homo sapiens*. But there are also limits to what in reality he tackles. He was likely aware that by his lifetime humans had gone from stone tools to telephones, from hunting and gathering to flying airplanes, from illiteracy to Shakespeare, from bows and arrows to poison gas. Still, the strenuous mental activity that led to the remarkable evolution of our species was initially peripheral to his interests. A great deal of how humans have lived and developed is mostly outside what he specifically includes in the reality principle.

Given his omissions, what does Freud actually mean by this concept? His 1911 essay "Formulations on the Two Principles of Mental Functioning" is the place to start. He begins by stating that "we are now confronted with the task of investigating...the relation of...mankind to reality" (Freud, 1958 [1911], SE XII, p. 218). For humans, the first primary process is "gaining pleasure" (Freud, 1958 [1911], SE XII, p. 219). This aim of obtaining satisfaction is "directed towards the external world" as the id presses "for immediate satisfaction at all costs" (Freud, 1959 [1927], SE XX, p. 201). When such demands and desires were not fulfilled "the psychical apparatus had to...form a conception of the real circumstances of the external world." The result was, according to Freud, the introduction of a "new principle of mental functioning...the *reality principle*," which "proved to be a momentous step" (Freud, 1958 [1911], SE XII, p. 219).

How so? For one it meant that the importance of "external reality" was "heightened." This included the centrality of "*consciousness*" which fostered impartial judgment that enabled determining if something agreed with reality or did not. Freud said this judgment entailed "the process of *thinking*." This thought process allowed the desire for pleasure to be postponed (Freud, 1958 [1911], SE XII, p. 221). It is interesting that Freud here focuses more on the thinking process involved with the reality principle than in what reality entailed. For if reality frustrated the pleasure principle, it would be important to know what are the components of reality. Freud though turns away from trying to understand reality to more practical concerns.

The first step to him is to learn to distinguish between what is internal from what "emanates from the outer world" (Freud, 1961 [1930], SE XXI, p. 67). This differentiation allows the "reality-ego" to strive "for what is *useful* and guard itself against damage." The reality principle does not depose the pleasure principle but is interested in "only a safeguarding of it" (Freud, 1958 [1911], SE XII, p. 223). In this conception, the reality principle is most interested in finding ways of preserving the pleasure principle. In other words, the reality principle in Freud has little interest in the fullness of reality.

He says that the function of the reality principle is for someone to postpone or abandon certain "sources of pleasure." That sacrifice entails becoming "'reasonable'" (Freud, 1963 [1916–1917], SE XVI, p. 357). As he says, it is the "pressure of external necessity" that leads one to "obey the reality principle" (Freud, 1963 [1916–1917], SE XVI, p. 371). Adhering to the reality principle has to do with the person's ego recognizing that the pleasure principle will not achieve satisfaction. One becomes reasonable by recognizing the obstacles to fulfillment and in some way postponing the desired pleasure. It could then be said one is being realistic. Clearly there is a difference between adjusting to practical necessity and what reality is. For to him the ego and its reality principle represent "reason and common sense" (Freud, 1961 [1923], SE XIX, p. 25). Freud's conception of thinking is mostly practical. It is ascertaining whether desiring something has a chance of being fulfilled or that reality will frustrate that desire. It is not about thinking as engaging with the complexities of the external world. The reality principle as Freud explains it then does not much illuminate the ways the real world impacts on psychic reality. This begs the question what in reality needs to be explained by his conception of the human mental structure?

Civilization and Sublimation

But later Freud shows more interest in reality itself. His most serious grappling with the intersection of the internal and external is in his 1930's *Civilization and Its Discontents*. What does he mean by civilization? To him, it serves the purposes of distinguishing humans from other animals, and "to protect men against nature and to adjust their mutual relations." This also includes the "cultural" phenomenon of inventing tools, controlling fire, and constructing dwellings. These activities are "useful to men for making the earth serviceable to them" (Freud, 1961 [1930], SE XXI, pp. 89–90).

Furthermore, Freud recognized that over the last few generations humankind has established a "control over nature in a way never before imagined." Freud mentions the railroad, telephone, how the advances of medicine have reduced infant mortality and lengthened the human life span (Freud, 1961 [1930], SE XXI, pp. 87–88). He finds that civilization encourages "man's higher mental activities – his intellectual, scientific and artistic achievements – and the leading role it assigns to ideas in human life" (Freud, 1961 [1930], SE XXI, p. 94). As these advances have transformed human existence, any conception of humanity's mental structures has to account for what has facilitated these extraordinary developments. As well, Freud had proclaimed psychoanalysis deals with normal life. Such normality in Freud's time and place of 20th-century Vienna included the railroad, telephone, automobile, movies, radio. airplanes, the Industrial Revolution, the high art in Vienna of literature, painting, music, the influential Vienna Circle in philosophy, and the quantum mechanics of 1933 Nobel Prize winner Erwin Schrödinger. Freud resided in a city where high culture was a regular feature of life. Could Freud's own psychoanalysis help explain how humanity could produce such splendors that permeated everyday life in his Vienna, among other locations?

In 1923, Freud portrays humanity as a species focused on the pleasures of the id, the restrictions of the super-ego, and adjusting expectations through adapting the reality principle. It is not evident in this structure where Freud systematically attempts to delineate how humanity's higher mental interests emerge. There is a related question, according to Freud, it is fairly recently that our major accomplishment occurred. But as a species *Homo sapiens* are hundreds of thousands of years old. Why is it that only in the last several centuries has humankind made such remarkable advances?

Freud never addresses what took us so long to become advanced. Still, there are two sometimes divergent concepts that Freud employs to explain humanity's accomplishments. One is sublimation which arises from desexualization and resides in the ego along with consciousness and the reality principle. The other is Eros, which derives from the Greek god of love, and is also connected to the activation of sexual love. One strand is desexualized and the other heightens sexuality.

Sublimation

First, can Freud's notions explain our miraculous innovations which have become crucial components of normal life in the industrial era? Not surprisingly, he attributes these higher activities to psychoanalytic notions. He finds that the ways in which civilization discourages direct satisfaction of the sexual instinct leads to sublimation, which entails finding substitutes for the restrictions on instinctual primal pleasure. For sublimation is based on "an abandonment of sexual aims, a desexualization" (Freud, 1961 [1923], SE XIX, p. 30). Freud declares "Sublimation of instinct…is what makes it possible for higher psychical activities, scientific, artistic or ideological, to play such an important part in civilized life" (Freud, 1961 [1930], SE XXI, p. 97). How so? To him sublimation may take "place regularly through the mediation of the ego." There is even an interconnection of sublimation with the life instincts. He writes, "*sublimated* energy" retains "the main purpose of Eros – that of uniting and binding" which moves toward "establishing the unity, or tendency to unity, which is particularly characteristic of the ego" (Freud, 1961 [1923], SE XIX, p. 45). To Freud, "*sublimation*" occurs after "the energy of the infantile wishful impulses" are "replaced by one that is higher, and perhaps no longer sexual" but that is "socially valuable. It is probable that we owe our highest cultural successes to the contributions of energy made in this way to our mental functions" (Freud, 1957 [1910], SE XI, pp, 53–54).

So far Freud assumes what needs to be explained. What needs to be comprehended is what in our mental/emotional makeup makes possible these higher cultural interests and capacities. There is nothing in Freud's concept of sublimation that distinguishes between becoming an excellent poker player or being the Wright brothers and learning how to fly the first airplane. Nor for that matter what leads some to propagate paranoid conspiracy theories and others to develop empirical criteria that can distinguish warranted factual conclusions from illusion His concept of sublimation when isolated does not get near to explaining the leap to what makes humans excel. Sublimation by itself is an underdeveloped, incomplete concept. It is not up to the task of carefully delineating what accounts for our higher mental faculties.

In seeking to understand our sophisticated mental capabilities, some other things might be helpful to consider. For sublimation within the ego to result in these high-level achievements, it would require intense and focused concentration. So more on what in consciousness might lead to advanced achievement should be again reviewed. To Freud, "consciousness….can receive excitations…from the perceptual system" (Freud, 1953 [1900], SE V, p. 574). To Freud, "Experience" shows that "as a rule ….a state of consciousness is characteristically very transitory; an idea that is conscious now is no longer a moment later" (Freud, 1961 [1923], SE XIX, p. 14). He repeats this observation in 1939. Then he writes, "consciousness is in general a highly fugitive state. What is conscious is conscious is conscious only for a moment" (Freud, 1964 [1939], SE XXIII, p. 159). This contrasts with his 1933 statement "that there are no sources of knowledge of the universe other than the intellectual working-over of carefully scrutinized observation" (Freud, 1964 [1933], SE XXII, p. 159). Again, Freud recognizes that humans can have extended consciousness and focus to make careful observations, but his theory of consciousness does not specifically identify what can lead from the transitory segments of consciousness to its highly focused capacities in science and other higher mental endeavors. So far neither his theory of sublimation nor of consciousness gets us from the unconscious to these clearly sensational advances in technology, science, the arts, and intellect. Again, he is not very thorough at demonstrating what allows humanity to excel in the external world.

How about what he says about thinking and thought? The "process of thinking…made it possible for the mental apparatus to tolerate an increased tension of stimulus while the process of discharge was postponed" (Freud, 1958 [1911], SE XII, p. 221). Here thinkings function is to deal with frustrations stemming from the pleasure principle, and is not specifically engaged with finding knowledge of the universe. Thinking when mentioned again, contains "one species of thought activity," which "remained subordinate to the pleasure principle alone" (Freud, 1958 [1911], SE XII, p. 222). This reaffirms that thought is more aimed at the id than external reality. It is also the case that Freud maintains that thought is not independent. To Freud, "the activity of thinking is…supplied from the sublimation of erotic motive forces" (Freud, 1961 [1923], SE XIX, p. 45).

Then he goes in a different direction. For to him what is both most low and the highest "can be unconscious." He asserts that "we have evidence that even subtle and difficult intellectual operations" can "equally be carried out preconsciously." Freud says this to counteract the belief that the "higher any mental function ranks… the more easily it will find access to consciousness" (Freud, 1961 [1923], SE XIX, pp. 27, 26). While he does specify how the unconscious process can occur during sleep, he does not show how the higher mental processes work while awake, nor why humans are interested in these activities. His treatment of thinking so far then does not aid in explaining how humanity has excelled in various higher order domains.

From thinking, he goes to empirical endeavors. To Freud, one of the accomplishments of science is to gain "insight" into "relations which are present in the external world" (Freud, 1964 [1940], SE XXIII, p. 196). He also specifies that humans possess "mind" and can be "intellectual" (Freud, 1964 [1940], SE XXIII, p. 114). Still, he has not sufficiently shown how thinking which is a product of sublimation actually emerges yet alone expands into the higher mental endeavors yet alone to the remarkable achievements of civilization. Again, he assumes what needs to be shown. For given the insufficiency within his explication of how sublimation works, it remains unclear how in the human mental structure we rise from the pleasure principle to the higher mental capacities.

Eros

Maybe his explication of Eros can get us farther. Eros, of course, was the Greek god of erotic love. Freud said that Eros and Thanatos were the two major instincts. It is hard to discuss one without including the other. The death instinct, Freud asserts, compels organic life to revert to being inorganic. To him, the aim of all life is death. This death instinct also in part expresses itself "as instinct of destruction" (Freud, 1961 [1923], SE XIX, pp. 40–41).

Eros for Freud has the following major components: the sexual instinct, instinctual impulses that are sublimated, and the self-preservative instinct (Freud, 1961 [1923], SE XIX, p. 40). There is a connection between "sexual instincts" which he "equated with life instincts" (Freud, 1955 [1920], SE XVIII, p. 53). Again, "the sexual instincts are the purest example of the...instincts of life" (Freud, 1955 [1921], SE XVIII, p. 102). He says that the self-preservative instinct is "certainly of an erotic kind." Still to maintain its existence it must also be aggressive (Freud, 1964 [1933], SE XXII, p. 209). As well, Eros for him has another function. It is to have "living substances" form "into ever greater unities" in order to have humans "brought into higher development" (Freud, 1955 [1923], p. 258). Here Freud is not only presenting Eros as an erotic instinct but one leading to unifying and in the process for humans to become higher and higher in achievements. Eros is a path to the greater scientific, technological, intellectual, and artistic heights that Freud recognizes and admires.

He earlier had proclaimed that he has "no faith ...in the existence of" some "instinct towards perfection at work in human beings" that has resulted in the "present high level of intellectual achievement." The impulse toward reaching the heights is "a result of the instinctual repression" which is the foundation for "all that is most precious in human civilization" (Freud, 1955 [1920], SE XVIII, p. 42). To him, the "highest goods of humanity" not only are "research, art, love, ethical and social sense" have "their origin in elementary and animal instinctual impulses" (Freud, 1955 [1923], p. 252). But the assertion that repression is the foundation for our high achievements is distinct from the life instinct of Eros and the erotic side of life. Freud is going in a variety of distinct directions at the same time. He does not integrate the repressive and the erotic. As well, it is not infrequent that Freud does not seek to specify the steps that go from the repressive to the capacity to achieve these highest endeavors. Why and how repression just does not remain the repressed and somehow gets channeled into higher mental activities is not really attempted, yet alone explained. Freud is content with the great leap he asserts between repression and humanity's highest achievements. As has been mentioned, he assumes what needs to be explained. Seeking to make sense of how humanity has become so advanced leads us into a Freudian jumble.

In September 1897 Freud chose to favor the internal world of fantasy over what transpires in material reality. When in 1930, he champions scientific, intellectual, artistic and technological splendors, his explication still flounders over the deep interconnection of psychic to external reality. He had in 1897 diminished what a child being sexually abused could mean, and was largely disinterested in the severity of what is now labeled adverse childhood experiences. Freud also underrepresented how post-traumatic stress resulting from combat can take over the psyche and body. In neither case did he bother to show the steps by which these traumas were diminished. He had the same problem of not being thorough in explaining how psychoanalysis could develop criteria to be scientific. Similarly, with how humans have become so advanced he left gap after gap after gap while proclaiming sublimation or Eros or the ego ideal could lead from the unconscious to conscious achievements of the highest order. All of these limitations were also revealing of the gaps between his focusing on the unconscious more than better connecting the internal and external. As Freud did not sufficiently appreciate how psychic reality can be infected by real traumatic experiences, he had similar difficulties in understanding what in being human has led us from being hunter gatherers to flying to the moon and inventing smart phones. His desire to stress fantasy over reality resulted in admirable, revolutionary discoveries and doctrines, that unfortunately too often are incomplete in both what is involved in the unconscious and the vital connection between the internal and external. Freud's efforts to explain how humanity has achieved so much is insufficient.

References

Freud, S. (1953). *The standard edition of the complete psychological works of Sigmund Freud, The Interpretation of Dreams, Volume V.* (J. Strachey, Ed. and Trans.). The Hogarth Press (Original work published 1900).

Freud, S. (1955). *Beyond the pleasure principles, The standard edition of the complete psychological works of Sigmund Freud Volume XVIII.* (J. Strachey, Ed. and Trans.). The Hogarth Press, pp. 7–64. (Original work published 1920).

Freud, S. (1955). *Group psychology and the analysis oof the ego, The standard edition of the complete psychological works of Sigmund Freud, Volume XVIII* (J. Strachey, Ed. and Trans.). The Hogarth Press, pp. 69–143. (Original work published 1921).

Freud, S. (1957). *Five lectures on psychoanalysis. The standard edition of the complete psychological works of Sigmund Freud, Volume XI* (J. Strachey, Ed. and Trans.). The Hogarth Press, pp. 9–54. (Original work published 1910).

Freud. S. (1957). The unconscious. *The standard edition of the complete psychological works of Sigmund Freud, Volume XIV* (J. Strachey, Ed. and Trans.). The Hogarth Press, pp. 166–215. (Original work published 1915).

Freud S. (1958). *Formulations on the Two Principles of Mental Functioning, The standard edition of the complete psychological works.* (J. Strachey, Ed. and Trans.). p. 218. The Hogarth Press, (Original Work published 1911).

Freud, S. (1959). Psycho-analysis. *The standard edition of the complete psychological works of Sigmund Freud, Volume XX* (J. Strachey, Ed. and Trans.). The Hogarth Press, pp. 263–270. (Original work published 1926).

Freud, S. (1961). *The ego and the id. The standard edition of the complete psychological works of Sigmund Freud, Volume XIX.* (J. Strachey Ed. and Trans.). The Hogarth Press, pp. 12–66. (Original work published 1923).

Freud, S. (1961). *Civilization and its discontents. The standard edition of the complete psychological works of Sigmund Freud, Volume XXI* (J. Strachey Ed. and Trans.). The Hogarth Press, pp. 64–125. (Original work published 1930).

Freud, S. (1963). *Introductory lectures on psycho-analysis (Part III). The standard edition of the complete psychological works.* (J. Strachey, Ed. and Trans.) p. 357. The Hogarth Press (Original work published 1916–1917).

Freud, S. (1964). *New introductory lectures on psycho-analysis. The standard edition of the complete psychological works of Sigmund Freud, Volume XXII* (J. Strachey Ed. and Trans.). The Hogarth Press, pp. 5–182. (Original work published 1933).

Freud S. (1964). Why war? *The standard edition of the complete psychological works of Sigmund Freud. Volume XXII.* (J. Strachey Ed. and Trans.). The Hogarth Press, pp. 197–220. (Original work published 1933).

Freud, S. (1964). *An outline of psycho-analysis. The standard edition of the complete psychological works of Sigmund Freud, Volume XXIII.* (J. Strachey Ed. and Trans.). The Hogarth Press, pp. 144–207. (Original work published 1939–1940).

Chapter 8

The Freudian Psychology of Love

As Eros is the god of love, might we learn some vital things about Dr Freud by discussing what he thinks about sex and romance? Concerning his ideas on love, both his strength and limitation is his emphasis on the underside, the unconscious sexually derived motivations in human relationships. Freud brings the discussion back to less altruistic notions of love. He grounds our emotional connection with others to their infantile sources, shows the sides of love that grow out of need, demand, desire, and complicated family dynamics. "I have never ventured beyond the ground floor and basement of the building," Sigmund Freud wrote in 1936 (Freud and Binswanger, 2003, p. 212). What makes Freud's perspective on love distinctive is his rooting it in early childhood relationships. For him, there is something that transpires to the youngster that has life-long impact on all that follows. He also centers love in interpersonal family dynamics. Freud sees the importance of the romantic dyad, but the couple is part of a larger network of connections, rivalries identifications, and jealousies. In describing family dynamics about love Freud demonstrates the connection between the internal and external in ways that are not always prominent in much of his other writing.

Still, disentangling love and sex is a challenge in Freud's work. Sex and aggression were the two basic drives, love is not included. In the index to his complete works, sexuality covers about five pages, love, a little more than a column. Still, what makes Freud so important for understanding the nature of love is his concentration on the earliest relationship, that of mother and infant. He sees this connection as the prototype for all subsequent romantic attachments. While Freud built on the 19th-century glorification of the mother, he moved this idealization from the mother as a moral force, to the mother as providing the nourishment-sensual-sexual-relational needs of the baby. He believed that the emotions aroused in infancy have long lasting impact on the individual's romantic life. As much as he revealed the centrality of the mother to the child, he did not omit the father's importance, or that of siblings. Through the notions of identification and object choice, he brought in the problem of gender and the importance of sexual identity. Attachment-separation issues and the vicissitudes of relationships also have strong roots in Freud's thought. Later investigators would show it is not just the feeding at the breast that forms the child, but also tactile touching, sensuality,

DOI: 10.4324/9781041074717-11

varying attachment patterns, stages of brain development, and the actual parent child relations that are important.

Love, Freud maintains, is when the mental side of sexuality is in the foreground (Freud, 1963 [1916–1917], SE XVI, p. 329). He believes the origins of love are in the satisfied need for nourishment (Freud, 1964 [1940], SE XXIII, p. 188). He sees sexual life beginning with the baby sucking the mother's breast (Freud, 1963 [1916–1917], SE XVI, p. 314). When "children fall asleep after being sated at the breast, they show an expression of blissful satisfaction which will be repeated in life after the experience of a sexual orgasm" (Freud, 1963 [1916–1917], SE XVI, p. 313). The mother finds fulfillment in relation to her baby. The

> mother's love for the infant she suckles and cares for....is in the nature of a completely satisfying love-relation, which not only fulfills every mental wish but also every physical need; and...it represents one of the forms of attainable human happiness.
>
> (Freud, 1957 [1910], SE XI, p. 117)

In feeding and sexually arousing the infant "lies the root of a mother's importance, without parallel, established unalterably for a whole lifetime as the first and strongest love-object and as the prototype of all later love-relations- for both sexes" (Freud, 1964 [1940], SE XXIII, p. 188). The mother is the child's first love object (Freud, 1963 [1916–1917], SE XVI, p. 329). When he speaks of an object choice, he means it is what one wants to have (Freud, 1955 [1921], SE XVIII, p. 106). Love then to Freud is involved with possessing the object, which at first is the mother.

The course of the child's love for the mother does not run smooth. While others attribute the disruption in the infant-mother bond to the child's anxiety over separation, Freud dates the crisis in the relationship to the appearance of a younger sibling. "A child," Freud writes,

> who has been put into second place by the birth of a brother or sister, and who is now for the first time almost isolated from his mother, does not easily forgive her this loss of place; feelings which in an adult would be described as greatly embittered arise in him and are often the basis of a permanent estrangement.
>
> (Freud, 1963 [1916–1917], SE XVI, p. 334)

This loss "of love" leaves behind "a permanent injury to self-regard in the form of a narcissistic scar" (Freud, 1955 [1920]. SE XVIII, p. 20). It is not only a baby sister or brother that stands between mother and child. The young boy observes that his father stands between him and his mother (Freud, 1955 [1921], SE XVIII, p. 105). "He does not forgive his mother for having granted the favour of sexual intercourse not to himself but to his father, and he regards it as an act of unfaithfulness" (Freud, 1957 [1910], SE XI, p. 171).

His displacement from his mother arouses the boy's anger, not at the unfaithful mother, Freud asserts, but toward his paternal rival. The son's relationship with his father "takes on a hostile coloring and becomes identical with the wish to replace his father in regard to his mother as well" (Freud, 1955 [1921], SE XVIII, p. 105). Freud's writing on the girl's Oedipal dynamics is not as extensive or clear as those on boys. Still from his writings, it is evident the little girl finds herself in emotional turmoil when she chooses her father as her desired love object and turns away from the mother who nourished and cared for her. To Freud, emotional attachment becomes complicated by rivalry for the love object's attention. Love desires exclusiveness, and from childhood on, this desire is difficult to fulfill. These issues emerge in the complete Oedipus complex, which Freud maintains, stems from the bisexuality present in children (Freud, 1961 [1923], SE XIX, p. 31). The Oedipal drama becomes a complicated triangle where the child struggles over gender and sexual identity. On the one hand, the child wants to possess the mother and get rid of the father, on the other the child wants to have the father and sees the mother as rival. The strength of the child's gender identification with one or the other parent determines whether the child chooses the positive Oedipus complex and the parent of the opposite sex as the love object, the negative complex where the youngster chooses the parent of the same sex as the love object, or some combination of the two (Freud, 1961 [1923], SE XIX, pp. 31–32).

While to many love is a dyadic relationship, Freud sees it at the minimum as being a triad. Competition and object choice go hand in hand. The lover is worried about being replaced by someone else, a rival for exclusive possession. Concern over whether one is loved or not is as much part of romance as is benevolence toward the loved object. Equally part of this Oedipal dynamic is sexual and gender identification. The complete Oedipus complex offers a spectrum of positive and negative object choices and identifications. This means that sexual identities can take a variety of forms within each individual and this internal diversity impacts on the outcome of the Oedipus complex and subsequent object choices. The dynamics of the complete Oedipus complex then show how individuals develop their sexual selves, what can stimulate romantic attraction, and how relational conflicts are implicit in dyadic love alliances. Freud believes that moving beyond romantic fixation on a parental object choice is important. "The liberation of an individual, as he grows up, from the authority of his parents is one of the most necessary though one of the most painful results brought about by the course of his development" (Freud, 1959 [1909], SE IX, p. 237). This may happen if incestuous fantasies can be overcome (Freud, 1953 [1905], SE VII, p. 227). The emergence of a super ego corresponds to the male child giving up his mother as a love choice.

Then after puberty, sexual love is front and center. For "love naturally consists… in sexual love with sexual union as its aim" (Freud, 1955 [1921]. SE XVIII, p. 90). Yet, according to another motif in Freud's writings, it is not always easy to let go of the first love choices. The "first allocations of the libido" are "powerful," later object choices do not quite measure up. "The husband is…only ever a substitute, never the right man….the father…has first claim on the woman's capacity for love, the husband has at best the second place" (Freud, 1957 [1918], SE XVII, p. 203). To Freud, these emotional complications indicate that "there is something in the nature of the sexual drive itself that is unfavorable to the achievement of complete satisfaction." An adult sexual partner is a "surrogate" for the original object choice, and a later choice cannot "bring full satisfaction" (Freud, 1957 [1912], SE XII, pp. 188–189).

The lover or spouse is always fighting ghosts from the nursery. Adult romances then contain echoes of childhood Oedipal object choices. The struggle for liberation from the parent's authority is likely never ending. Neither philia, agape, Platonic Eros, nor Shakespearean constancy can explain these complex undercurrents of romantic entanglements that Freud reveals. It is in showing these relational complications, with their roots in infancy and the Oedipus complex, that Freud makes his major contribution to understanding the dynamics of love. He redirects discussion about love away from the one-sided emphasis on benevolence and goodness in philia and agape to the vagaries of attachment and object choice.

While literature can illustrate the volatility of romance, Freud's ideas go farther in showing why sexual connections arouse such a range of emotions. There is a double-sidedness in Freud's writing here. On the one hand he writes that "the Oedipus complex...is bound to pass away...when the next pre-ordained phrase of development sets in." On the other hand, the individual never gives up the first love object and Oedipal longings follow him or her through the rest of life (Freud, 1961 [1924], SE XIX, p. 174).

A similar tension permeates his writings on love, a word he says which is "exceedingly ambiguous" (Freud, 1959 [1925], SE XX, p. 38). As Freud writes, love is the mental side of sexual life. How he views the intermixture of love and adult sexuality is important for the meaning of his ideas. On the one hand, he discusses the mutuality of love; on the other hand, he presents it as primarily sexual and self-seeking. The "word 'love'" concerns the "synthesis of all the component instincts of sexuality under the primacy of the genitals and in the service of the reproductive function" (Freud, 1957 [1915], SE XIV, p. 138). Freud, as mentioned, has phrased this slightly differently a few years later: "what we mean by love naturally consists...in sexual love with sexual union as its aim" (Freud, 1955 [1921], SE XVIII, p. 90). Sexual intercourse seeks pleasure and yet is "subordinated to the reproductive function" (Freud, 1953 [1905], SEVII, p. 207). In normal love, the affectionate and sensual are combined (Freud, 1957 [1912], SE XII, p. 180).

Reference has been made to the bliss after orgasm. In a clinical manner, Freud describes the male side of intercourse, which begins with producing a pleasurable excitement, then results in "the discharge of the sexual substances." After the great final sexual pleasure, "the tension of the libido is for the time being extinguished" (Freud, 1953 [1905], SE VII, p. 210). Individual acts of sexual union may be ecstatic, but overall the sexual drive may not be fulfilling. This is for two reasons. As mentioned, the original object choice of a parent is not obtainable, and no substitute is as treasured as the parent. The excremental and sexual are intertwined to each other and this is aesthetically displeasing (Freud, 1957 [1912], SE XII, pp. 189–190). The sexual act itself cannot be separated from its relational and physical connotations. The legacy of our first love-sexual preferences shapes the road to romance and makes it conflicted and not totally fulfilling. As well, in Freud's explication, this is not about a mutually shared peak experience, nor about female fulfillment. It is about the male sexual encounter.

Nevertheless, for him the sexual drive propels humans toward romantic encounters. The sexual, along with the libidinal and life instincts, is what Freud calls Eros, and whose aims are unification and the prolonging of life (Freud, 1955 [1923], SE XIX, p. 258). The Greek word Eros, Freud writes, is just a translation of the German word for love. Freud also says: "Psychoanalysis, then, gives these love instincts the name of sexual instincts" (Freud, 1955 [1921], SE XVIII, p. 91). Besides driving people to the sex act, libido can be diverted from or prevented from reaching its aim (Freud, 1955 [1921], SE XVIII, pp. 90–91).

Like a hit and run driver, Freud connects love to Eros, philia, agape, and then expounds little on how these sublimations and diversions are outgrowths of the sex drive, particularly as they relate to seeking the well-being of the loved ones. In Freud, the line between sex and love can be murky and undeveloped. He needs to further explicate what is the nature of parental love and love for humanity, and how the sexual drive becomes altruistic. For Freud does not present parental love as concerned with the well-being of the child. "Parental love…is nothing but the parents' narcissism born again" (Freud, 1957 [1914], SE XIV, p. 91). Overall, in not extending Eros to wishing the fulfillment and best interests of the partner, Freud has a too narrow understanding of Eros. For eroticism may lead to love as within and beyond sexual fulfillment. A deep erotic bond often naturally may evolve into a component of mutuality, give and take, a full, if complex partnership in all aspects of being. This conception of Eros is not a Freudian one. His theory remains more within an individual's psyche than a primordial, deep, long lasting dyadic bond. It is as much about the individual psyche than the interpersonal relationship.

Not surprisingly the issue of the other as a being in and for themselves is problematic in Freud's writings. He does make an attempt to distinguish between any act of sexual intercourse and romance. Freud writes: "the difference between an ordinary object-cathexis and the state of being in love is that in the latter…the ego empties itself as it were in favour of the object" (Freud, 1961 [1927], SE XXI, pp. 164–165). When "we are in love a considerable amount of narcissistic libido overflows on to the object….the object serves as a substitute for some unattained ego ideal of our own" (Freud, 1955 [1921], SE XVIII, p. 112). These quotes are self-referential to the lover. They say little about the loved one other than how they connect back to the ego and attachments of the lover. Philosopher Irving Singer: "According to Freud, all love…every interest in another object is just a circuitous device for satisfying self-love" (Singer, 1984, p. 29).

There are other dimensions to these relationships. Loving and being loved, it might be argued, are intermixed in love relationships. Feeling loved includes being tended to, having personal and sexual needs fulfilled, and one's inner core reached. Loving another involves a free bestowal of affection and care, an interconnection even immersion in the life of the loved one. It may not qualify as true love, though, until commitment to the well-being of the loved one in and of itself permeates the emotions and actions of the lover. This benevolence is mixed with the other rough and tumble entanglements, unconscious wishes, and inevitable mixed motivations of intimate attachments. As Freud's conception of love does not incorporate deep care for the other's best interest, his writings do not reach the level of benevolent love.

To illustrate the self-referential side of his version of what love is, let's return to Freud's clinical description of the sexual act in *Three Essays on Sexuality*. He mentions the stimulation of the penis and the vagina, which brings excitement and leads to male sexual matter being emitted. "This last pleasure is the highest in intensity," Freud writes. Once the discharge occurs "the tension of the libido is for the time being extinguished" (Freud, 1953[1905], SE VII, p. 210). This account of a sexual union is male centered. While the female partner's sexual responses are alluded to, they are not developed. Also, there is not any discussion of the mutual feelings that may have occurred as male and female are joined together in this intimate experience. Again, the sense of a lover being a partner is absent here, as it is in much of Freud's explication of the erotic.

Freud describes the object choice as someone to have, not with whom to be and share. Even when Freud discusses the early over-valuation of the loved object, his references are to the feelings of the lover and not the being and well-being of the loved one. A parallel pattern exists within Freud's explication of the Oedipus complex. While Freud recognizes that the father and mother have sexual feelings for the child, he does not show that the shape the child's complex takes is a result of a mutually interactive triadic system. Instead, he reverts to declaring that the origins of the complex remain within the desires of the child. The shape and course of the complete Oedipus complex then is presented as the struggles over gender identity within the child, and not also as part of the actual relationship and dynamics between all the parties.

There is another wrinkle. When the Freudian youngster selects the mother as the first love object, the child has a personal response to the flesh and blood individual who has her own traits and characteristics. Later during the inner struggles of the complete Oedipus complex, Freud says that the outcome is dependent on the strength of competing sexual identifications. He does not stress the way the child internalizes the mother's traits through the perspective of his or her own temperament. In real life, the individual is both a child of the parents and their own being.

When after puberty the time comes to fall in love, the romantic partners may both repeat old patterns and create new ones. Freud worries though that subsequent love partners cannot equal the idealized first childhood love choice of mother or father. But the parent has not been faithful; mother or father has allegiances to spouse or another child. The youngster is left rejected, estranged, scarred. Later in life, he or she may seek a lover who will be more faithful and true. The danger is that they will reenact the pattern adapted after initially feeling abandoned and scorned.

To the questions, what is love, what are the various kinds of love, what enhances and what undermines love, and what is the connection/conflict between marital and parental love, Freud is helpful in some regards and not in others. What can sustain and what undermine romance is hinted at but not developed in his work, nor does he elaborate on non-sexual love. If Freud had seen more that the drive for sexual union can also be mutual sharing, and the object choice and identification can mean not only having and being like but being with and truly caring for the other's well-being, he may have been able to give a rounded portrait of love, its development, its joys and tribulations. Mixing the more benevolent and more self-seeking sides of romance might also have led him to address some of the issues of love's longevity, and different dimensions in the conflicting loyalties between marital and parental love.

What is striking is the difference between how Freud handles bonds and rivalries in childhood, and what he describes after puberty. Then there is less on the interpersonal, and more on the intrapsychic. With adult sexuality and love, he reverts to the separation of the internal and external that mars his theories in general. In what in adult pair bonding is most intimate and mutual is not Freud's central focus. The diverse dynamics within actual adult love relationships is not a subject he in detail addresses.

References

Freud, S. (1953). *Three essays on the theory of sexuality. The standard edition of the complete psychological works, Vol. VII,* (J. Strachey Ed. and Trans.). The Hogarth Press, pp. 130–245 (Original work published 1905).

Freud, S. (1955). *Beyond the pleasure principle. The standard edition of the complete psychological works, Vol. XVIII* (J. Strachey Ed. and Trans.). The Hogarth Press, pp. 7–64 (Original work published 1920).

Freud, S. (1955). *Group psychology and the analysis of the ego. The standard edition of the complete psychological works, Vol. XVIII* (J. Strachey Ed. and Trans.). The Hogarth Press, pp. 69–143 (Original work published 1921).

Freud, S. (1955). Two encyclopedia articles. *The standard edition of the complete psychological works, Vol. XVIII* (J. Strachey Ed. and Trans.). The Hogarth Press, pp. 235–259 (Original work published 1923).

Freud, S. (1957a). A special type of object choice made by men. *The standard edition of the complete psychological works, Vol. XI* (J. Strachey Ed. and Trans.). The Hogarth Press, pp. 165–175 (Original work published 1910).

Freud, S. (1957b). Leonardo da Vinci and a memory of his childhood. *The standard edition of the complete psychological works, Vol. XI* (J. Strachey Ed. and Trans.). The Hogarth Press, pp. 63–137 (Original work published 1910).

Freud, S. (1957). On the universal tendency to debasement in the sphere of love. *The standard edition of the complete psychological works, Vol. XI* (J. Strachey Ed. and Trans.). The Hogarth Press, pp. 179–190 (Original work published 1912).

Freud, S. (1957). On narcissism: An introduction. *The standard edition of the complete psychological works, Vol. XIV* (J. Strachey Ed. and Trans.). The Hogarth Press, pp. 73–102 (Original work published 1914).

Freud, S. (1957). Instincts and their vicissitudes. *The standard edition of the complete psychological works, Vol. XIV* (J. Strachey Ed. and Trans.). The Hogarth Press, pp. 117–140 (Original work published 1915).

Freud, S. (1957). The taboo of virginity. *The standard edition of the complete psychological works, Vol. XI,* (J. Strachey Ed. and Trans.). The Hogarth Press, pp. 193–208 (Original work published 1918).

Freud, S. (1959). Family romances. *The standard edition of the complete psychological works, Vol. IX* (J. Strachey Ed. and Trans.). The Hogarth Press, pp. 237–241 (Original work published 1925].

Freud, S. (1959). An autobiographical study. *The standard edition of the complete psychological works of Sigmund Freud, Vol. XX* (J. Strachey Ed. and Trans.). The Hogarth Press, pp. 1–71. (Original work published 1925).

Freud, S. (1961) *The Ego and the Id, The standard edition of the complete psychological works, Vol. XIX* (J. Strachey Ed. and Trans.). The Hogarth Press, pp. 12–66 (Original work published 1923).

Freud, S. (1961). The dissolution of the Oedipus complex. *The standard edition of the complete psychological works, Vol. XIX* (J. Strachey Ed. and Trans.). The Hogarth Press, pp. 175–179 (Original work published 1924).

Freud, S. (1961). Humour. *The standard edition of the complete psychological works, Vol. XXI* (J. Strachey Ed. and Trans.). The Hogarth Press, pp. 164–165. (Original work published 1927).

Freud, S. (1963). *Introductory lectures on psycho-analysis, Part III. The standard edition of the complete psychological works, Vol. XVI* (J. Strachey Ed. and Trans.). The Hogarth Press, pp. 73–102 (Original work published 1914).

Freud, S. (1964). *An outline of psycho-Analysis. The standard edition of the complete psychological works, Vol. XXIII* (J. Strachey Ed. and Trans.). The Hogarth Press (original work published 1940).

Freud S. and Binswanger, L. (2003). *The Sigmund Freud-Ludwig Binswanger correspondence 1908–1938.* Other Press (Original letter 1936).

Singer, I. (1984). *The nature of love, Volume 1. Plato to Luther.* University of Chicago Press.

Chapter 9

What Does Freud Mean by the Oedipus Complex?

In this last chapter, I return to what was earlier addressed. With the Oedipus complex, Freud diverted attention away from the father's perversions to the son's sexual desires. In Freud's more than 40 years of discussing Oedipal issues his divisions over the internal and external contributed to a lack of a unified Oedipal theory. Others have noticed this. French analysts Laplanche and Pontalis point out, "Freud himself nowhere gives any systematic account of the Oedipus complex" (Laplanche and Pontalis, 1973, p. 283). The "Oedipus complex is elaborate and elusive," according to prominent psychoanalyst Jay Greenberg, "... it contains a large number of related but logically independent propositions" (Greenberg, 1991, p. 6). Seymour Fisher and Roger Greenberg concur. "Freud's Oedipal concepts" are not "unidimensional," they write. Instead, "his Oedipal theory is actually a string of theories about a wide sweep of developmental issues" (Fisher and Greenberg, 1996, pp. 160–161). Simon arid Blass observe that "Freud's ideas on the Oedipus complex...change, the terminology is changed, the scope of what is to be considered oedipal is constricted and expanded" (Simon and Blass, 1991, p. 161).

Sigmund Freud himself in letters said things that reinforced these concerns. Freud confessed that "an all embracing synthesis never has been the important issue" (Hale, 1971, p. 190). For the "systematic working through of material is not possible for me; the fragmentary nature of my experience and the sporadic character of my insights do not permit it" (Freud and Andreas-Salome, 1972, p. 95). Freud himself admitted that his "explanations are unsystematic and full of gaps" (Hale, 1971, p. 90).

These recognitions did not stop Freud from making the boldest declarations about the Oedipus complex. "Every new arrival on this planet," he writes, "is faced with the task of mastering the Oedipus complex" (Freud, 1953 [1905], footnote added note 1920, SE VII, p. 226). To Freud, "the *Oedipus complex*...in every human being is of the greatest importance in determining the final shape of his erotic life" (Freud, 1961 [1923], SE XIX, p. 245). He adds that "mankind as a whole may have acquired the sense of guilt...at the beginning of its history...in connection with the Oedipus complex" (Freud, 1963 [1916–1917], SE XVI, p. 332). The "beginnings of religion, morals, society and art converge in the Oedipus complex" (Freud, 1955 [1913], SE XIII, p. 156).). For "the Oedipus complex may justly be regarded as the nucleus of the neuroses" (Freud, 1963 [1916–1917], SE XVI, p. 337).

DOI: 10.4324/9781041074717-12

Given these convictions, Freud conceived four developmental stages to the Oedipus complex. First, there is what he calls the pre-Oedipus period. Second, the complex itself, with all its complications, emerges during the phallic stage; third, according to Freud, it normally gets resolved at the end of this period and is succeeded by the super-ego and the latency period. Finally, during puberty the Oedipus complex gets reactivated and has its subsequent impact on the erotic and social life of humankind. What follows is his perspectives on the four stages of the Oedipus complex.

Pre-Oedipal

The first developmental stages are combined in the pre-Oedipal period. He begins with the biological fact that the "young of the human race pass through a long period of dependence and are slow in reaching maturity" (Freud, 1955 [1919b], SE XVIII, p. 261). It is within families that children are raised, and the mother is the central caregiver for most infants. First, the mother is the infant's "first protection against all the undefined dangers which threaten it" (Freud, 1961 [1927], SE XXI, p. 24). Second, for Freud the most crucial aspect of the mother's relationship is her feeding of her baby. The "mother, who satisfies the child's hunger becomes its first love-object" (Freud, 1961 [1927], SE XXI, p. 24). "A child's first erotic object is the mother's breast that nourishes it" (Freud, 1964 [1940], SE XXIII, p. 188). "Sucking at the mother's breast," Freud writes, "is the starting-point of the whole of sexual life. The unmatched prototype of every later sexual satisfaction... This sucking involves making the mother's breast the first object of the sexual instinct" (Freud, 1963 [1916–1917], SE XVI, p. 314). Third, there is pleasure in the act of feeding. According to Freud,

an infant will repeat the action of taking nourishment without making a demand for further food... We describe this as sensual sucking... the fact of the act of sensual sucking has in itself alone brought him satisfaction...infants perform actions which have no purpose other than obtaining pleasure.
(Freud, 1963 [1916–1917], SE XVI, pp. 313–314)

Fourth, as Freud writes, "love has its origin in attachment to the satisfied need for nourishment" (Freud, 1964 [1940], SE XXIII, p. 188). "We call the mother the first love-object" (Freud, 1963 [1916–1917], SE XVI, p. 329). In caring for the child's body and arousing the child sexually "lies the root of a mother's importance, unique, without parallel, established unalterably for a whole lifetime as the first and strongest love-object and as the prototype of all later love-relations- for both sexes" (Freud, 1964 [1940], SE XXIII, p. 188). In selecting the "mother as a love-object everything becomes attached which, under the name of the 'Oedipus complex,' has attained so much importance in... psycho-analytic explanation" (Freud, 1963 [1916–1917], SE XVI, p. 329).

In his earlier writings, Freud assumed a parallel development for both sexes and thought that biology dictated that boys love their mothers and girls their fathers.

Toward the end of his career, he reversed himself and claimed that the mother is the first object choice for both sexes. The pleasures of being nourished, the cognitive recognition of the difference between self and other, and the phylogenetic imagination all lead to the infant's choice of mother as love object for male and female in early infancy.

Freud recognizes that not all mothers breast-feed and that not all breast-feeding is done by mothers. He says that the child's first sexual object is the person who does the feeding, caring and protecting whether it is the "mother or a substitute for her" (Freud, 1957 [1914], SE XIV, p. 87). But then later he declares that the "figure of the wet nurse who suckles the child is as a rule merged into the mother" (Freud, 1964 [1933], SE XXII, p. 122). To Freud "it makes no difference whether a child has really sucked at the breast or has been brought up on the bottle and never enjoyed the tenderness of a mother's care…the child's development takes the same path." This is because, as previously noted, what Freud calls the "phylogenetic foundation has … the upper hand over personal accidental experience" (Freud, 1964 [1940], SE XXIII, pp. 188–189). In this way, mothers become the universal first sexual object for all children, male and female alike, no matter who nurtured them in infancy. The foundation of the Oedipus complex is in having the mother be the sexual object choice of every child. The die is cast; sexuality and the internal psychological state of the child are in the foreground.

Another important element in Freud's discussion of the pre-Oedipal period are the concepts of identification and object choice. To Freud, "identification … is what one would like to be." He distinguishes this from object choice which is "what one would like to have" (Freud, 1955 [1921], SE XVIII, p. 106). In identification, there is

> the assimilation of one ego to another one, as a result of which the first ego behaves like the second in certain respects, imitates it and in a sense takes it up into itself… It is a very important form of attachment… probably the very first, and not the same thing as the choice of an object… Identification and object-choice are to a large extent independent of each other.
>
> (Freud, 1964 [1933], SE XXII, p. 63)

Freud makes other broad generalizations. "A little boy," Freud explains, "will exhibit a special interest in his father; he would like to grow like him and be like him… he takes his father as his ideal" (Freud, 1955 [1921], SE XVIII, p. 105). A female's pre-Oedipal "identification with her mother… rests on her affectionate attachment to her mother and takes her as a model" (Freud, 1964 [1933], SE XXII, p. 134).

But we run into Freud's changing views. Freud's contention that identification is the first emotional connection to another is not consistent with what he said about the impact on the child of being nourished by his mother. A breast-fed child will have definite knowledge of crucial distinction between the sexes, because the child at some point knows who takes it to the breast for nourishment and who does not. In 1923, Freud wrote: "At the very beginning, in the individual's primitive oral phase, object-cathexis and identification are no doubt indistinguishable from each other" (Freud, 1961 [1923], SE XIX, p. 29). Identification would then begin with the mother, who is the child's first object choice. Freud cannot quite make up his mind between declaring that the child's first attachment is to the mother, then the father, then both. We begin to see why psychoanalytic observers and Freud himself recognize incompletions and gaps in the crucial phenomenon of the Oedipus complex.

For some reason Freud also feels he has to make one parent more important to the psychic life of the infant than the other. But he vacillates between making the mother then the father more important to the youngster. As a result, there is confusion in his concept of identification and the relationship of identification and object choice. In particular, Freud has trouble with cross-gender identification. In discussing the pre-Oedipal period, he does not show the meaning for the girl of identifying with her father, or for the boy of taking his mother as a model. As such, his theory of identification contains a significant gap. We can see how parts of his Oedipal theory are all over the place.

While clearly his attempt to establish the priority of mother or father as attachment figures is conceptually muddled, he does make clear that identification and object choice follow different courses for male and female. At this early time in her life, "a little girl's father is not much else for her than a troublesome rival" (Freud, 1961 [1931], SE XXI, p. 226). The girl has a unified psychology; her object choice and her identification are with the same person, her mother.

It is different for the pre-Oedipal boy who is the eldest son. At first, he saw the mother as his protector, but the mother "is soon replaced by the stronger father, who retains that position for the rest of childhood" (Freud, 1961 [1927], SE XXI, p. 24). The "earliest years' of childhood 'are dominated by an enormous overvaluation of his father" (Freud, 1964 [1939], SE XXIII, p. 12). The son identifies with his father as his hero. Yet at

> the same time as this identification with his father, or a little later, the boy has begun to develop a true object-cathexis towards his mother...He...exhibits... two psychologically distinct ties: a straightforward sexual object-cathexis towards his mother and an identification with his father...The two subsist side by side for a time without any mutual influence or interference.
>
> (Freud, 1955 [1921], SE XVIII, p. 105)

There is an additional complication in the pre-Oedipal period. While boys and girls are selecting a love object and a model, mothers and fathers have their own agendas in relation to their offspring. "The parents," Freud writes, obey "the pull of sexual attraction" (Freud, 1963 [1916–1917], SE XVI, p. 333). Mothers favor male over female children. To Freud, the relation between "mother and son...provides the purest example of an unchangeable affection, unimpaired by any egoistic considerations" (Freud, 1963 [1915–1916], SE XV, p. 207). "A mother is only brought unlimited satisfaction by her relation to a son; this is altogether the most perfect, the most free from ambivalence of all human relationships" (Freud, 1964 [1933], SE XXII, p. 133).

The mother is not the only parent with a favorite. "The father will give the plainest evidence of his greater affection for his little daughter" (Freud, 1963 [1916–1917], SE XVI, p. 333). While the pre-Oedipal boy may not feel divided by his love for his mother and admiration for his father, the same could not be said for his father. "In the happiest young marriage," Freud writes, "the father is aware that the…baby son…has become his rival, and this is the beginning of an antagonism towards the favorite" (Freud, 1957 [1910b], SE XI, p. 117). Not surprisingly, Freud makes the choices of mother and father into a broad uniform generalization. Still, he here does not fully extend these statements about the parents to an analysis of the full psychological ramifications of family life. He throws out hints of the complex web of family dynamics, but goes no further. Even though Freud discussed Oedipal dynamics for over four decades, developing a coherent account of this phenomenon so far has not been a strong point.

Phallic Stage and Oedipus Complex

The second period in Freud's conception of the Oedipus complex is the phallic stage, which ushers in the Oedipus complex proper. Freud writes: "from the third year of life onwards at about that time the genitals already begin to stir, a period of infantile masturbation-of genital satisfaction… sets in" (Freud, 1963 [1916–1917], SE XVI, p. 325). He calls this the phallic stage for both boys and girl because he considers the primary sexual organs of this period to resemble the phallus: the penis in the boy and the clitoris in the female. What Freud calls the positive or normal Oedipus complex emerges when the boy, desiring his mother begins to see his father as a rival, and the girl switches allegiance and takes her father as her object choice and develops hostile feelings toward her mother. Thus emerges "the triangular character of the Oedipus situation" (Freud, 1961 [1923], SE XIX, p. 31).

Between the age of three and five, a change in the child occurs which plunges the child into the midst of complex and conflicting feelings. "The little boy," Freud writes, "notices that his father stands in his way with his mother. His identification with his father then takes on a hostile coloring and becomes identical with the wish to replace his father in regard to his mother as well" (Freud, 1955 [1921], SE XVIII, p. 105). The boy's desire to get rid of his father is one side of a two-sided attitude. "The hatred of his father that arises in a boy from rivalry for his mother is not able to achieve uninhibited sway over his mind; it has to contend against his old established affection and admiration for the very same person. The child finds" himself in "conflict" due to "this ambivalent emotional attitude towards his father" (Freud, 1955 [1913], SE XIII, p. 129). Similarly, the little girl finds herself in emotional turmoil when she chooses her father as her desired love object and turns away from the mother who nourished and cared for her.

For the boy, the mother as well as the father stands in the way of the fulfillment of Oedipal desires. The son is painfully aware that his mother has chosen his father over him as a mate. When Freud formulates the Oedipus complex, he stresses the son's love for the mother and jealousy of the father, but not the boy's grievances toward the mother. This is despite the fact that the Oedipal son considers it to be "an act of unfaithfulness" that his mother has "sexual intercourse" with "his father" (Freud, 1957 [1910a], SE XI, p. 171). The birth of a younger sibling is "unmistakable proof of the infidelity of the' mother and leads to the son feeling 'scorned'" (Freud, 1955 [1920], SE XVIII, p. 21). The "child grudges the unwanted intruder and rival...and develops a grievance against the faithless mother" (Freud, 1964 [1933], SE XXII, p. 123).

Grievance, yes. But the boy's animosity for some strange reason is stronger toward the father, even though it is the mother who chooses to sleep with her husband. Why then by this logic would Oedipal dynamics still have the boy choosing his mother as a sexual object choice who in his mind betrayed their love by rejecting the son and choosing the father. It is not explained how it would work psychologically for the boy to both choose his mother as his love object and suffer a narcissistic scar when she rejects him for his father or a newborn sibling. Here is one of the central explanatory gaps in Freud's exposition of the phallic stage. The mother's psychic divisions between son and husband also would fly in the face of his declaration that the mother's connection to her son is the freest from ambivalence of all human relationships.

On the subject of mothers, Freud biographer Peter Gay comments that Freud "seems to have dealt with the conflicts that his complicated feelings towards his mother generated by refusing to deal with them" (Gay, 1988, p. 506). While Freud gives place to the Oedipal boy's mixed emotions toward his father, Freud does not know how to include the male child's hostile feelings toward his mother into his conception of how the Oedipus complex works.

When Freud later deals with this subject matter in his notion of the positive and negative Oedipus complex, he again focuses on one parent as the object choice and the other as rival. There is, according to Freud, a positive, a negative and a complete Oedipus complex. The positive one entails love for the parent of the opposite sex and hostility toward the same-sex parent. In the negative Oedipus complex, "a boy... wants to take his mother's place as the love-object of his father" (Freud, 1955 [1925b], SE XX, p. 250). Freud says: "the identification with the father has become the precursor of an object-tie with the father. The same holds good, with the necessary substitutions, of the baby daughter as well" (Freud, 1955 [1921], SE XVIII, p. 106). The complete Oedipus complex,

which is...positive and negative... is due to the bisexuality originally present in children...a boy has not merely an ambivalent attitude towards his father and an affectionate object-choice towards his mother, but at the same time he also behaves like a girl and displays an affectionate feminine attitude to his father and a corresponding jealousy and hostility towards his mother.

(Freud, 1961 [1923], SE XX, p. 33)

Freud stays with the choice of one parent as object and the other as rival despite the grievance either a boy or girl would have if they choose one parent while the other has betrayed them in the marital bed.

Freud's explication of the positive and negative Oedipus complex and this phenomenon as a whole makes another assumption. The Oedipus complex itself is supposed to be a triad of mother, father and child. But, as Freud knows, not all families have both parents and there are often additional children, there are extended families, other kinds of family structures and some children are raised from birth in orphanages. Freud has a variety of ways, not all of them consistent with each other, of accounting for these differences.

So how does Freud explain these things? He does recognize that in many cultures that the sexes are segregated; women live with women and men with men. So, there are families without fathers and without fathers present. Freud sees this as having a strong impact on the son's development. "The absence of a strong father in childhood not infrequently favors the occurrence of inversion" (Freud, 1953 [1905], footnote added 1915, SE VII, p. 146). He writes: "it almost seems as though the presence of a strong father would ensure that the son made the correct decision in his choice of object, namely someone of the opposite sex" (Freud, 1957 [1910b], SE XI, p. 99). To Freud, "the presence of both parents plays an important part" among the "factors that influence object-choice" (Freud, 1953 [1905], footnote added 1915, SE VII, p. 146). But he also has asserted that in Leonardo da Vinci's case, there was no father present, and this benefited the boy. Leonardo's "later scientific research, with all its boldness and independence, pre-supposed the existence of infantile sexual research uninhibited by his father" (Freud, 1957 [1910b], SE XI, p. 123). From this perspective, accidental experience significantly affects a child's identity and the outcome of their Oedipal struggles. Again, Freud's theories on the Oedipus complex moves in opposite directions.

Freud even goes so far as to assert that given the mother's unfaithfulness, the boy "may take his sister as a love-object by way of substitute for his faithless mother" (Freud, 1963 [1916–1917], SE XVI, p. 334). This is not just a whim. As Freud writes: "A human being's first choice of an object is regularly an incestuous one, aimed, in the case of the male, at his mother and sister" (Freud, 1963 [1916–1917], SE XVI, p. 335). As well, a "little girl may find in her elder brother a substitute for her father who no longer takes an affectionate interest in her" (Freud, 1963 [1916–1917], SE XVI, p. 334).

Then there is the case of Napoleon and his older brother, Joseph. Freud writes:

The elder brother is the natural rival; the younger one feels for him an elemental, unfathomably deep hostility for which... the expressions 'death wish' and 'murderous intent' may be found appropriate. To eliminate Joseph, to take his place...must have been Napoleon's strongest emotion as a small child.

(Freud, 1960, pp. 432–433)

The hostility toward Joseph that Freud attributes to Napoleon is parallel to the jealousy sons usually feel toward their father in the Oedipal period. That Napoleon was the second son, then, according to Freud, made a significant difference in Napoleon's emotional life. With these variations on Oedipal dynamics, we see again how family structure and dynamics may deviate from proclaiming the Oedipus complex is just a triad. We can see how the theory of the Oedipus complex is a jumble of inconsistencies and underexplored dynamics.

As well, Freud is not completely comfortable with a model that gives such prominence to experience. He proposes another model, based more on heredity, one that might account for some of the gaps in the Oedipus complex. A phylogenetic inheritance, Freud maintains, is the legacy of all human beings and influences how an individual responds to particular events. Again,

> The reactions to early trauma...are not strictly limited to what the subject himself has really experienced but diverge from it in a way which fits...the model of a phylogenetic event...the behavior in the Oedipus...complex abounds in such reactions, which seem unjustified in the individual case and only make sense phylogenetically - by their connection with the experience of earlier generations.
> (Freud, 1964 [1939], SE XXIII, p. 99)

To Freud,

> primal phantasies...are a phylogenetic endowment. In them the individual reaches beyond his own experience into primeval experience at points where his own experience has been too rudimentary...children in their phantasies are simply filling in the gaps in individual truth with prehistoric truth.
> (Freud, 1963 [1916–1917], SE XVI, p. 371)

He adds: "Wherever experiences fail to fit in with the hereditary schema, they become remodeled in the imagination" (Freud, 1955 [1918], SE XVII, p. 119). For example, a nurse becomes fused with the mother for the child. Thus, the mother becomes the child's object choice, even if it was the wet nurse rather than the mother who nourished and protected the child. Due to the phylogenetic inheritance, the diversity of human circumstances and experiences becomes a single pattern. The phylogenetically inherited schemata make possible the universality of primal phantasies and, thus, the universality of the triad of the Oedipus complex.

On the one hand, Freud gives a prominent place to the actual dynamics within family life. On the other hand, he denies them all by giving precedence to the phylogenetic inheritance. These tensions within the Oedipus complex mirror Freud's divisions between experience and inheritance that resulted in his favoring the biological predispositions Overall, Freud has trouble bringing together the intersection of the internal and external factors, the biological and the experiential, in the shaping of the Oedipus complex in the phallic period.

Dissolution of the Oedipus Complex

The third period concerns the initial resolution of the Oedipus complex. Freud gives two accounts of what leads to its dissolution, one he calls ontogenetic and the other phylogenetic. Ontogenetically, "the Oedipus complex would go to its destruction from its lack of success, from the effects of its internal impossibility" (Freud, 1961 [1924b], SE XIX, p. 173). On the phylogenetic side, Freud declares that

> the Oedipus complex must collapse because the time has come for its disintegration, just as the milk-teeth fall out when the permanent ones begin to grow ... the Oedipus complex ... is determined and laid down by heredity and which is bound to pass away according to programme when the next pre-ordained phase of development sets in.
>
> (Freud, 1961 [1924b], SE XIX, p. 174)

He sees these views as compatible (Freud, 1961 [1924b], SE XIX, p. 174).

To resolve the positive Oedipus complex, the boy, according to Freud, would need to abandon his mother as love object and reduce his hostility to his father; the girl will need to stop hating her mother and expecting to marry her father. Ontogenetically, there is much in the actual experience of the child in the family that leads to the younger one feeling rejected by the love object:

> The early efflorescence of infantile sexual life is doomed to extinction because its wishes are incompatible with reality and the inadequate stage of development which the child has reached...The tie of affection, which binds the child as a rule to the parent of the opposite sex, succumbs to disappointment, to a vain expectation of satisfaction or to jealousy over the birth of a new baby - unmistakable proof of the infidelity of the object of the child's affection.
>
> (Freud, 1955 [1920], SE XVIII, pp. 20–21)

After the arrival of a sibling, the boy feels in "second place" in relation to his mother. He becomes "greatly embittered" and often this leads to "a permanent estrangement...A little girl may find...her father...no longer takes an affectionate interest in her as he did in her earliest years" (Freud, 1963 [1916–1917], SE XVI, p. 334). Both boys and girls feel displaced. Freud says: "distressing experiences of this sort...are inevitable" (Freud, 1961 [1924b], SE XIX, p. 173). The disappointment that accompanies these experiences has significant emotional consequences. As mentioned, the result is "a permanent injury to self-regard in the form of a narcissistic scar" (Freud, 1955 [1920], SE XVIII, p. 20). For both boy and girl alike, "the absence of the satisfaction hoped for...lead the small lover to turn away from this hopeless longing" (Freud, 1961 [1924b], SE XIX, p. 173). The Oedipal love object is abandoned because of unfaithfulness, being displaced, feeling estranged, rejected and hopeless. Actual experiences can account for the child turning away from the opposite sex parent as object choice or even finding a replacement within the family. But Freud also has an alternative view of how the love object is given up. One that is more phylogenetic.

To Freud, the little boy, during this period, turns to his genitals and finds sexual pleasure in playing with them. Adults do not approve of masturbation. To get him to stop, "a threat is pronounced that this part of him which he values so highly will be taken away from him. Usually, it is from women that the threat emanates" (Freud, 1961 [1924b], SE XIX, p. 174). However, the phylogenetically inherited schema remodels experience. In writing about one of his male clients, Freud declares that though the castration threats to him "emanated from women…it was his father from whom…he came to fear castration…heredity triumphed over accidental experience" (Freud, 1955 [1918b], SE XVII, p. 86).

Initially, "the boy does not believe in the threat or obey it in the least" (Freud, 1961 [1924b], SE XIX, p. 175). Freud writes that it is only when the boy-child actually sees a naked female that the threat of castration becomes real. When he views "the genital region of the little girl," he "cannot help being convinced of the absence of a penis in a creature who is so like himself" (Freud, 1961 [1924b], SE XIX, p. 176). The boy concludes, "little girls too had a penis, but it was cut off and in its place was left a wound" (Freud, 1957 [1910b], SE XI, p. 95). After that recognition, when once again he hears:

the threat that the organ which is so dear to him will be taken away from him if he shows his interest in it too plainly. Under the influence of this threat of castration he now sees the notion he has gained of the female genitals in a new light, henceforth he will tremble for his masculinity.

(Freud, 1957 [1910b], SE XI, p. 95)

Freud asserts:

If the satisfaction of love in the field of the Oedipus complex is to cost the child his penis, a conflict is bound to arise between his narcissistic interest in that part of his body and the libidinal cathexis of his parental objects. In this conflict the first of these forces normally triumphs; the child's ego turns away from the Oedipus complex.

(Freud, 1961 [1924b], SE XIX, p. 176)

How Freud knows that most frequently it is a female who threatens castration is difficult to understand. As often happens Freud makes factual statements without conducting or citing empirical research. Nor does Freud adequately explain why the phylogenetic inheritance includes fear of being castrated by the father. How does he know either of these things? But again, the ways he uses the notion of the phylogenetic inheritance enables him to avoid human diversity. Certainly, there can be homes where there are no females and only males, or only females and no fathers or other males.

Freud also has another explanation that is made possible by his 1923 presentation of the human mental structure. The authority of the father or parents is
introjected into the ego, and there it forms the nucleus of the super-ego, which
takes over the severity of the father and perpetuates his prohibition against
incest...The libidinal trends belonging to the Oedipus complex are in part
desexualized...and changed into impulses of affection....This process ushers in
the latency period, which now interrupts the child's sexual development.

(Freud, 1961 [1924b], SE XIX, pp. 176–177)

In this process, sexual development comes to a standstill and the latency period
begins (Freud, 1959 [1926a], SE XIX, p. 108). Again, this seems more phylogenetic than ontogenetic, as there are numerous families without a father or father
figure in the home.

The castration complex ends both the positive and negative Oedipus complex
of the young male, lead to identification with the father and the emergence of the
super-ego. Through the "intensification of his identification with his father...the
dissolution of the Oedipus complex would consolidate the masculinity in a boy's
character" (Freud, 1961 [1923], SE XIX, p. 32). He adds, "At the dissolution of
the Oedipus complex, there is a father-identification and a mother-identification...
The relative intensity of the two identifications in any individual will reflect the
predominance in him of one or the other of the two sexual dispositions" (Freud,
1961 [1923], SE XIX, p. 34).

In both sexes the relative strength of the masculine and feminine sexual dispositions is what determines whether the outcome of the Oedipus situation shall be
an identification with the father or with the mother (Freud, 1961 [1923], SE XIX,
p. 33).

But there is also needed an explanation for why some males choose other men
as partners, and why some females become lesbians. The phylogenetic inheritance
supposedly remodels actual occurrences to fit in with the pre-ordained schema that
has males identifying with their father. But in relationship to the male homosexual,
the inherited sexual predisposition and the phylogenetic schema are in conflict. It
is not clear from Freud's writings whether sexual disposition is a necessary or sufficient condition for the development of homosexuality. In any case, the result is
that the castration complex by itself does not explain the sexual identification of
the son, and thus is not sufficient to explain the dissolution of the Oedipus complex.
Neither the ontogenetic nor the phylogenetic factors convincingly show how all
male children leave the Oedipus complex behind and move into the latency period.

There remains though a tension between the ontogenetic and the phylogenetic. On
the phylogenetic side, the boy would turn away in disgust from castrated females.
Ontogenetically, the birth of younger siblings causes the boy to feel displaced
and to turn away in anger and sorrow from his mother as a chosen love object.
Freud has claimed that both Napoleon and himself saw their older brothers as their
chief rivals and directed their hostility toward them. But, none of this ontogenetic
side should matter. According to Freud, the phylogenetic schema should remodel

experience to fit in with our inheritance. So, neither Freud nor Napoleon should have their brothers as their primary rivals. But, according to Freud, they did. In these cases, Freud is presenting instances where the ontogenetic side prevailed, and the phylogenetic side did not wipe out these actual experiences.

He has also said that the child's position in the family is of "extreme importance" in shaping his life (Freud, 1963 [1916–1917], SE XVI, p. 334). If so, Freud would need to more systematically explore these dynamics. But Freud does not fully consider how family structure and size impact on how the Oedipus complex is resolved. With both the ontogenetic and phylogenetic version of the dissolution, it is assumed that all people who have Oedipus complex resolve them for this period during this third stage. So again, the diversity of external experience is not front and center in Freud's thinking. Still, his theory of the resolution of the male Oedipus complex may account for the positive Oedipus complex, but does not account for how the negative, complete, nor family complexes, nor the emergence of homosexuality or bisexuality are always resolved within the Oedipus complex. Disparities within Freud's formulation of the Oedipus complex are present in all such stages Freud has elucidated.

The Female Oedipus Complex in the Phallic Stage

For decades, observers have noticed that Freud is more male than female centered. Does he do well in discussing the female Oedipus complex? Freud does not maintain, as Jung did, that there is an Oedipus complex for boys and an Electra complex for girls. Freud though believes males and females are different and that the path to the Oedipus complex diverges for males and females.

He asserts that the positive Oedipus complex for the girl would be love for the father and rivalry with the mother. For Freud the question is "how does a girl pass from her mother to an attachment to her father... to which she is biologically destined?" (Freud, 1964 [1933], SE XXII, p. 119). Freud gives an ontogenetic and a phylogenetic version of how this switch occurs.

Ontogenetically, Freud says that the girl's "attachment to the mother is bound to perish, precisely because it was the first and was so intense...the attitude of love probably comes to grief from the disappointments that are unavoidable and from the accumulation of occasions for aggression" (Freud, 1961 [1931], SE XXI, p. 234). Anger and disappointment stem from the mother disciplining the child and from the birth of a younger brother or sister. When a younger sibling is born, the child "feels that it has been dethroned, despoiled, prejudiced in its rights; it casts a jealous hatred upon the new baby and develops a grievance against the faithless mother" (Freud, 1964 [1933], SE XXII, p. 123).

The "girl's strongest motive for turning away from her" mother is "that her mother did not give her a proper penis - that is to say, brought her into the world as a female" (Freud, 1961 [1931], SE XXI, p. 234). Freud assumes that for the girl the absence of the male organ means that she sees herself as castrated and develops a female castration complex. "The castration complex of girls," Freud declares, "is…started by the sight of the genitals of the other sex" (Freud, 1964 [1933], SE XXII, p. 125). He continues: "The discovery that she is castrated is a turning-point in a girl's growth…Her self-love is mortified by the comparison with the boy's far superior equipment" (Freud, 1964 [1933], SE XXII, p. 126). A girl "feels seriously wronged" and develops an "'envy for the penis'" (Freud, 1964 [1933], SE XXII, p. 125). A "consequence of penis-envy seems to be a loosening of the girl's affectionate relation with her maternal object…the girl's mother…is almost always held responsible for her lack of a penis" (Freud, 1961 [1925b], SE XIX, p. 254). For "with the discovery that her mother is castrated it becomes possible to drop her as an object, so that the motives for hostility…gain the upper hand" (Freud, 1964 [1933], SE XXII, pp. 126–127). Freud says that "the attachment to the mother ends in hate" (Freud, 1964 [1933], SE XXII, p. 121).

The girl's desire to have a penis, Freud asserts, turns her toward her father in a particular way. She wishes to give her father a baby. In doing so, the young girl "gives up her wish for a penis and puts in place of it a wish for a child and *with that purpose in view* she takes her father as a love-object" (Freud, 1961 [1925b], SE XIX, p. 56). "With the transference of the wish for a penis-baby, the girl has entered the Oedipus complex. Her hostility to her mother…is now greatly intensified, for she becomes the girl's rival" (Freud, 1964 [1933], SE XXII, p. 129). As the daughter and the mother compete for the father's affection, the Oedipal girl develops a negative identification with her mother. She "seeks to get rid of her mother and take her place with her father" (Freud, 1964 [1933], SE XXII, p. 134). Both components of the positive Oedipus complex are now in place, jealousy of the mother and desire for the father. The girl has moved from a negative to a positive Oedipus complex.

Freud's next task is to show how the female positive Oedipus complex is resolved, as he has declared that the Oedipus complex disintegrates when the next pre-ordained stage develops (Freud, 1961 [1924b], SE XIX, p. 173). The incentive for the boy to abandon the Oedipus complex is his fear of castration. But girls, according to Freud, already believe they have been castrated. Thus, for

girls the motive for the demolition of the Oedipus complex is lacking…Thus the Oedipus complex escapes the fate which it meets in boys; it may be slowly abandoned or dealt with by repression, or its effects may persist far into women's normal mental life.

(Freud, 1961 [1925b], SE XIX, p. 257)

Girls remain in' the Oedipus complex "for an indeterminate length of time; they demolish it late and, even so, incompletely. In these circumstances the formation of the super-ego must suffer; it cannot attain the strength and independence which gives it its cultural significance" (Freud, 1964 [1933], SE XXII, p. 129). To Freud, "for women the level of what is ethically normal is different for what it is in men. Their super-ego is never so inexorable, so impersonal…as what we require it to be in men" (Freud, 1961 [1925b], SE XIX, p. 257). Females then to Freud are less morally developed than males.

Freud also finds that for boys the Oedipus complex is destined to fade away, but not so for girls. It is not quite clear if the female Oedipus complex dissolves at all; and if it does, Freud does not fully explain how. The male castration complex leads to the demolition of the male positive Oedipus complex. The female castration complex cannot destroy the female Oedipus complex. So, Freud's declaration that the girl's Oedipus complex is demolished late and incompletely is not backed up by any real explanation of how this occurs. The only hint at an explanation he gives is ontogenetic. "One has an impression," Freud writes, "that the Oedipus complex is then gradually given up because this wish is never fulfilled" (Freud, 1961 [1924b], SE XIX, p. 179). This can occur at any time or at no particular time and Freud gives no indication of what mental realization would lead a girl to abandon her Oedipal phantasies. Similarly, he assumes a female super-ego, but does not explain how such a mental structure develops.

Freud has said that every human being faces the task of resolving the Oedipus complex. Females cannot easily make this resolution due to the anatomical distinction between the sexes. In this sense, Freud is saying there are two Oedipus complexes, one for males and another for females. The emergence of the male super-ego is preceded by the castration complex leading to a renewal of the boy's identification with his father. The castration complex only emerges after the little boy has seen the female genitals. But a boy may never have the opportunity to see a girl's private parts. The same may occur for girls. Freud assumes it is factual that a girl will see a penis, but there are reasons to believe that this need not be a universal occurrence. As has been mentioned, Freud is prone to assume facts not in evidence. Similarly, he does not consider that some girls who see a penis might prefer their own anatomy and that of grown women's appearance to that of boys and/or men.

The only way Freud envisions the development of an inexorable super-ego is by fear of losing a penis. As females have no penis to lose, there seems then, in Freud's thought, to be no positive incentive for girls to renounce Oedipal wishes for a baby from their father, nor any reason why they would develop a super- ego. They would remain in the Oedipal phase for an indefinite period. Anatomy may be destiny, but there is no inherited reason for the girl to move from the Oedipal to the latency period.

Yet somehow many girls do develop into women choose love-objects other than their fathers, marry and become mothers. Freud does give some indication of how this process can occur; it is by the female reverting to her pre-Oedipal identification with her mother. In her earlier years, the girl has "an affectionate attachment to her mother and takes her as a model" (Freud, 1964 [1933], SE XXII, p. 134). This "pre-Oedipus attachment is the decisive one for a woman's future: during it preparations are made for the acquisition of the characteristics with which she will later fulfill her role in the sexual function and perform her invaluable social tasks" (Freud, 1964 [1933], SE XXII, p. 134).

Characteristically, Freud does not indicate how the girl overcomes her anger at her mother for not providing her with a penis and her rivalry with the mother for the father's affection. He just asserts that under "the influence of a woman's becoming a mother, herself, an identification with her own mother may be revived" (Freud, 1964 [1933], SE XXII, p. 133). Of course, there is the obvious gap between the Oedipal desire for the father and the desire to take on the maternal role with some male outside her family of origin. Of course, Freud is giving one perspective where girls are unable to resolve their Oedipus complex and another where they can. His attempt to present a unified picture of female development moves in conflicting directions. On his own terms, he does not demonstrate a coherent development and resolution of the female Oedipus complex in the phallic stage. So, neither in relationship to all males nor all females is Freud able to show that the Oedipus complex is resolved or dissolved, nor that the positive Oedipus complex is a universal phenomenon.

The Oedipus Complex in Adolescence and Adulthood

But there is still more. To Freud, there is a latency period in childhood that is succeeded by puberty. During adolescence, according to Freud, the Oedipus complex is revived and then continues to have a major impact on individuals in adulthood and for civilization in general. He writes:

> the sexual life of man…comes on in two waves…It reaches a first maximum in the fourth or fifth year of a child's life…the sexual impulses…are overcome by repression, and a *period of latency* follows…At puberty the impulses and object-relations of a child's early years become re-animated and amongst them the emotional ties of his Oedipus complex.
>
> (Freud, 1955 [1925a], SE XX, p. 37)

Freud believes that "a person's final sexual attitude is not decided until after puberty" (Freud, 1953 [1905], footnote added 1915, SE VII, p. 225)

During adolescence, Freud writes: "the sexual life of maturing youth is almost entirely restricted to indulging in phantasies…In these phantasies, the infantile tendencies invariably emerge once more….the son being drawn towards his mother and the daughter towards her father" (Freud, 1953 [1905], SE VII, pp. 225–227).

What curtails the adolescent from carrying through these desires is a societal prohibition. In "the postponing of sexual maturation, time has been gained in which the child can erect…the barrier against incest….Respect for this barrier is essentially a cultural demand made by society" (Freud, 1953 [1905], SE VII, p. 225). As is typical, he assumes without evidence that all societies have adopted these sexual prohibitions and do so in a uniform manner in all cultures. He turns to the incest taboo, which was acquired historically and "has no doubt already become established in many persons by organic inheritance" (Freud, 1953 [1905], footnote added 1915, SE VII, p. 225).

He also has another challenge, heterosexuality. "One of the tasks implicit in object-choice," Freud writes in 1905, "is that it should find its way to the opposite sex. This, as we know, is not accomplished without a certain amount of fumbling" (Freud, 1953 [1905], SE VII, p. 229). As emotions and identifications in relation to the parents can move in a variety of directions, some people will not have opposite sex partners. Freud recognizes that "inversion...answers fully to the sexual inclinations of no small number of people" (Freud, 1953 [1905], SE VII, p. 229).

At the same time as he recognizes homosexuality, he still generalizes about the choice of being heterosexual, and connects it to ties to parents. For Freud the Oedipus complex lives on in the sexual life of adults. A wife is a mother-substitute and a husband cannot match a father in the eyes of a woman. As such, he now says that from puberty on, all heterosexual males and females are beholden to their Oedipal desires and cannot ever find a satisfying mate.

Is this another way of echoing the Old Testament declaration that the sins of the parents are passed on from generation to generation? "Mankind," Freud wrote in old age, "never lives entirely in the present. The past, the tradition of the race and of the people, lives on...and yields only slowly to the influences of the present and to new changes" (Freud, 1964 [1933], SE XXII, p. 67). To Freud, romance in adult life takes on many of the characteristics of the family complex, in that the individual may choose someone other than the parent as an object, but the emotions and wounds of the initial object choice are ever present. Even though the final sexual attitude congeals after puberty, the effects of infantile sexual life resonate throughout the life span. The extra-familial romantic partners that the adolescent and adult choose derives from their childhood object-choices within the family. The adult transfers the emotions from the Oedipal period to the new romantic partners.

But that again is not applied consistently in his writings. For he also envisions the opposite. For "these plainly incestuous phantasies are overcome and repudiated." How does this get accomplished? A "fundamental aim" of the institutions of "civic life," is "the enabling of the individual to master his Oedipus complex and to divert his libido from its infantile attachments into the societal ones that are ultimately desired" (Freud, 1961 [1924c], SE XIX, p. 208). For "the overcoming of the Oedipus complex coincides with the most efficient way of mastering the archaic, animal heritage of humanity" (Freud, 1955 [1919b], SE XVII, pp. 261–262). What is unfortunate is that while Freud maintains the necessity of overcoming early Oedipal ties, he also asserts that in heterosexual choices they are not dissolved. To Freud, the process of resolving the Oedipus complex and adjusting to social demands is never complete for "incestuous wishes... have never been fully overcome" (Freud, 1959 [1926b], SE XX, p. 214).

Once again, Freud is torn. On the one hand, he sees social progress tied to the emancipation of the individual from the parent's authority and the resolution of the Oedipus complex. On the other hand, Oedipal desires do not cease; they permeate society and limit the extent to which liberation is possible. With the fate of the Oedipus complex, Freud is drawn to irreconcilable doctrines that reflect his divided intellectual mind. Throughout his post 1897 writings, strong theoretical divisions mark his theories.

Conclusion

Freud's deep conceptual confusions permeate his expositions of the meaning of the Oedipus complex. The foundation is supposed to be the triangular relationship of children to their parents. However, the child's emotions of desire, jealousy, and rage that are integral to the Oedipus complex are also directed at other family members. According to Freud, a same-sex older sibling can even replace the parent as the child's rival for the opposite sex parent. The Oedipus complex need not be just a triad, nor restrained to the child's relationship to parents. In Freud's writings, it is not always quite clear how many and which people are involved in the Oedipus complex.

His theories of the Oedipus complex also go off in a variety of directions. The phylogenetic inheritance should ensure the universality and uniformity of the Oedipus complex. But lo and behold, the fact of bisexuality and the existence of the family complex reveal that the Oedipus complex is manifest in diverse ways. The castration complex with its roots in phylogeny, does not guarantee the dissolution of the Oedipus complex, as Freud asserts. An inherited sexual disposition may keep some males in the thralls of the negative Oedipus complex and so never resolve their Oedipus complex. Females, who Freud says already feel castrated, may not easily complete their Oedipus complex and move on to the next stage.

What is observable in Freud's theories is that he brings in external factors without leading him to revise his conception that the Oedipus complex as a triad is forced upon us by nature. But he is uninterested in recognizing that there can be diverse rather than universal reactions among males and females. When he generalizes about the post puberty question of the dissolution of the Oedipus complex, he moves in opposite directions simultaneously, and he does so primarily on internal factors while not fully considering how the external may impact on the internal. His Oedipal conceptions, as mentioned, are a jumble.

Sigmund Freud is one of the more original and distinctive thinkers in the Western Canon. But integrating the various components of his concepts is not his strong point. Anyone sympathetic to Freud's project must confront the fragmentary nature of his thought. To move forward Freud's divisions and contradictions must be acknowledged and sorted out. Freud is confounded by questions of etiology. Does the phylogenetic inheritance reshape experience to fit into its schema or can sexual disposition or a peculiarity of a family's dynamics alter what was formed in humankind's prehistory? Is anatomy destiny or are sexual constitutions so varied that the line between male and female psychology is not easily ascertained? Is the Oedipus complex determined by the family structure or is it independent of the existence and shape of the family? To what extent is the Oedipus complex a product of intrapsychic and/or interactive developments?

It may seem that Freud is so deeply divided that there is no way to resolve these issues. The Oedipus complex itself can be seen as a series of concepts that cannot be reconciled. I believe there is a core of value in the Oedipus complex. One of Freud's great strengths is his recognition of the importance of infancy, of how dependency and desire, attachment and identification influence the baby's psychological development. But then Freud loses his way. He makes contradictory statements about who has priority in the child's psyche: the mother through nourishment and object choice or the father through identification and the mantle of authority. He even is confused on whether all children identify first with both parents or whether the father is the first choice. It is unfortunate that Freud's conception of identification is so muddled. For the notion of identification as who a child wants to be like can give vitality and cohesion to the Oedipus complex.

Gender issues are problematic for Freud. He wants to elevate the role of the father, but then reluctantly recognizes that identification in the pre-phallic period is with both parents. But he does not carry this realization through. Even though he affirms bisexuality as an inherent part of the human psyche, he remains stuck in stereotypes of males as active and females as passive. The very same Freud who envisions mothers as the unmatched prototype of love for both sexes cannot bring himself to apply his theories equally to men and women.

The limitations of Freud's theorizing are unfortunate. For in the Oedipus complex, he attempts something that most of his successors do not. He strives to integrate the mother, the father and the family into the early psychological development of the child. Too often in post-Freudian psychoanalytic theory, the mother-infant relationship is isolated in a way that removes the baby from the full context of family and culture. Freud, for all his confusions, recognizes the importance of both parents, the centrality of the family complex, and that the child assimilates social values through the authority of the parents. In other words, the seeds of a theory of psychological development are contained within the Freudian Oedipus complex. Freud was unable to work through his intellectual divisions and develop a clear conception of the Oedipus complex, but he left the rudiments of an idea that can help us understand some of our deeper conflicts.

References

Fisher, S. and Greenberg, R. (1996). *Freud scientifically reappraised: Testing the theories and therapy.* John Wiley & Sons.

Freud, S. (1953). *Three essays on the theory of sexuality. The standard edition of the complete psychological works, Vol. VII* (J. Strachey Ed. and Trans.). The Hogarth Press, pp. 125–248 (Original work published 1905).

Freud, S. (1955). *Totem and Taboo. The standard edition of the complete psychological works, Vol. XIII* (J. Strachey Ed. and Trans.). The Hogarth Press, pp. 1–161 (Original work published 1913).

Freud, S. (1955). From the history of an infantile neurosis. *The standard edition of the complete psychological works, Vol. XVII* (J. Strachey Ed. and Trans.). The Hogarth Press, pp. 3–123 (Original work published 1918).

Freud, S. (1955). A child is being beaten. *The standard edition of the complete psychological works, Vol. XVII* (J. Strachey Ed. and Trans.). The Hogarth Press, pp. 175–204 (Original work published 1919a).

Freud, S. (1955). Preface to Reik's 'Ritual: Psycho-analytic studies.' *The standard edition of the complete psychological works, Vol. XVII* (J. Strachey Ed. and Trans.). The Hogarth Press, pp. 257–263 (Original work published 1919b).

Freud, S. (1955). *Beyond the pleasure principle. The standard edition of the complete psychological works, Vol. XVIII* (J. Strachey Ed. and Trans.). The Hogarth Press, pp. 3–64 (Original work published 1920).

Freud, S. (1955). *Group psychology and the analysis of the ego. The standard edition of the complete psychological works, Vol. XVIII* (J. Strachey Ed. and Trans.). The Hogarth Press, pp. 67–143 (Original work published 1921).

Freud, S. (1955). Some Psychical Consequences of the Anatomical Distinction Between the Sexes, *The standard edition of the complete psychological works, Vol. XIX.* (J. Strachey, Ed. and Trans.). p. 250. The Hogarth Press (Original work published 1925).

Freud, S. (1955). The question of lay analysis. *The standard edition of the complete psychological works of Sigmund Freud, Vol. XX* (J. Strachey, Ed. and Trans.). The Hogarth Press, pp. 177–250. (Original Work published 1926).

Freud, S. (1957). A special type of object-choice made by men. *The standard edition of the complete psychological works, Vol. XI* (J. Strachey Ed. and Trans.). The Hogarth Press, pp. 165–175 (Original work published 1910a).

Freud, S. (1957). *Leonardo da Vinci and a memory of his childhood. The standard edition of the complete psychological works, Vol. XI* (J. Strachey Ed. and Trans.). The Hogarth Press, pp. 59–137 (Original work published 1910b).

Freud, S. (1957). On narcissism. *The standard edition of the complete psychological works, Vol. XIV* (J. Strachey Ed. and Trans.). The Hogarth Press, pp. 67–102 (Original work published 1914).

Freud, S. (1959). *Inhibitions, symptoms and anxiety. The standard edition of the complete psychological works, Vol. XX* (J. Strachey Ed. and Trans.). The Hogarth Press, pp. 77–175 (Original work published 1926).

Freud, S. (1960). *Letters of Sigmund Freud* (E. Freud Ed.). Basic Books.

Freud, S. (1960). *The psychopathology of everyday life. The standard edition of the complete psychological works, Vol. VI* (J. Strachey Ed. and Trans.). The Hogarth Press (Original work published 1901).

Freud, S. (1961). *The ego and the id. The standard edition of the complete psychological works, Vol. XIX* (J. Strachey Ed. and Trans.). The Hogarth Press, pp. 3–66 (Original work published 1923).

Freud, S. (1961). The dissolution of the Oedipus complex. *The standard edition of the complete psychological works, Vol. XIX* (J. Strachey Ed. and Trans.). The Hogarth Press, pp. 172–179 (Original work published 1924b).

Freud, S. (1961). A short account of psycho-analysis. *The standard edition of the complete psychological works, Vol. XIX* (J. Strachey Ed. and Trans.). The Hogarth Press, pp. 191–209 (Original work published 1924c).

Freud, S. (1961). Some psychical consequences of the anatomical differences between the sexes. *The standard edition of the complete psychological works, Vol. XIX* (J. Strachey Ed. and Trans.). The Hogarth Press, pp. 243–258 (Original work published 1925).

Freud, S. (1961). *The future of an illusion. The standard edition of the complete psychological works, Vol. XXI* (J. Strachey Ed. and Trans.). The Hogarth Press, pp. 3–56 (Original work published 1927).

Freud, S. (1961). Female sexuality. *The standard edition of the complete psychological works, Vol. XXI* (J. Strachey Ed. and Trans.). The Hogarth Press, pp. 223–243 (Original work published 1931).

Freud, S. (1963).*Introductory lectures on psycho-analysis. The standard edition of the complete psychological works, Vol. XVI.* (J. Strachey, Ed. and Trans.). pp. 313–314, 332. The Hogarth Press (Original work published 1916–1917)

Freud, S. (1964). *New introductory lectures on psycho-analysis. The standard edition of the complete psychological works, Vol. XXII* (J. Strachey Ed. and Trans.). The Hogarth Press, pp. 3–182 (Original work published 1933).

Freud, S. (1964). *Moses and monotheism. The standard edition of the complete psychological works, Vol. XXIII* (J. Strachey Ed. and Trans.). The Hogarth Press, pp. 3–137 (Original work published 1939).

Freud, S. (1964). *An outline of psycho-analysis. The standard edition of the complete psychological works, Vol. XXIII* (J. Strachey Ed. and Trans.). The Hogarth Press, pp. 141–207 (Original work published 1940).

Freud, S. and Andreas-Salome, L. (1972). *Letters* (E. Pfeiffer Ed.). W.W. Norton.

Gay, P. (1988). *Freud: A life for our time.* W. W. Norton.

Greenberg, J. (1991). *Oedipus and beyond: A clinical theory.* Harvard University Press.

Hale Jr., N. (1971). *James Jackson Putnam and psychoanalysis: Letters between Putnam and Sigmund Freud, Ernest Jones, William James, Sandor Ferenczi and Morton Prince, 1877–1917.* Harvard University Press.

Laplanche J. and Pontalis, J. B. (1973). *The language of psycho-analysis.* W. W. Norton.

Simon, B. and Blass, R. (1991). The development and vicissitudes of Freud's ideas on the Oedipus complex. *The Cambridge companion to Freud* (J. Neu Ed.). P. 161. Cambridge University Press.

Index

Adler, A. 46
adolescence 30, 102–103
agape 83, 84
aggression 16, 49, 80, 99
Anderson, J. 1, 21
Anzieu, D. 26

Beeby, B. 68
Beller, S. 29
Bergmann, M. 64, 69
Bettelheim, B. 28
biology, and experience 53; Freud's
    inconsistencies about 54–55; inheritance
    enhances psychoanalytic universals
    59–61; phylogenetic inheritance
    and psychoanalytic psyche 56–59;
    psychoanalytic autonomy 54–56
bisexuality 99, 104
Blass, R. 88
Boesky, D. 64, 69
breast-feeding 60, 80–81, 89–90
Breger, L. 10
Breuer, J. 16
Brome, V. 43
brother-sister relationship 13, 94
Butterworth, B. 19

castration 60, 97–100, 104
childhood sexual abuse 2, 13–14, 19–21
Chodorow, N. 17
civilization 74–75
Civilization and Its Discontents (Freud)
    71, 74
Clark, R. 26, 28–29
consciousness 71, 73, 76
criticism, on Freud's methods 4, 63–64

Darwin, C. 57
Decker, H. 28

deferred obedience 40
The Development of the Unconscious Mind
    (Schore) 68
Devereux, G. 15–16
Dundes, A. 43, 44

Edelson, M. 64
ego 49, 72
The Ego and the Id (Freud) 72
Einstein, A. 64
Eissler, K. 11, 18
elder brother, as rival 33, 47, 60, 94–95,
    98–99
Electra complex 99
Eros 5, 75, 77–78, 80, 84
exclusive possession 27, 31, 82
external reality 17–18; childhood sexual
    abuse 19–21; war trauma 18–19

family: dynamics 2, 33, 80, 92, 104;
    romance 25–32, 35
fantasy 2, 4, 78; and reality 13–14, 17–18,
    78; unconscious 13–14, 16
father-daughter relationship 2, 5, 92–93,
    100, 102
father-son dynamics 12, 29, 35, 42
Ferenczi, S. 45, 47
Fisher, S. 88
Fliess, W., Freud's letters to 11–13, 31, 32, 47
"Formulations on the Two Principles of
    Mental Functioning" 73
Freiberg, Freuds at 25–26, 30, 32
Freud, Amalie (mother) 25
Freud, and fathers struggles 9–10;
    accusations 11–12; childhood sexual
    abuse 10–14, 19–21; internal fantasy
    and external reality 17–18, 78; Oedipus
    and, Laius 14–17; war trauma 3, 18–19
Freud, Anna (sister) 26–29

Freud, Emmanuel (half-brother) 11, 25
Freudian psychoanalysis 3, 64–68;
    civilization 74–75; and civilization's
    achievement 77–78; Eros 77–78;
    post-Freudian 68–69; reality principle
    73–74; sublimation 74–77
Freud, Jakob (father) 2, 9; psychological
    divisions 4, 6, 18; and Sigmund 10–14
Freud, Martin (son) 28, 29
Freud, Mathilde (daughter) 12, 14
Freud, Philipp (half-brother) 11, 25, 33
Freud, Sally Kanner (Jakob Freud wife) 25
Freud, Sigmund 24; and Alfred Adler
    conflicts 46–47; being a Jew 29–30;
    causes of hysteria 24, 30, 35; *Civilization
    and Its Discontents* 71, 74; creativity
    from former followers 49; *The Ego
    and the Id* 72; family romance 25–32,
    39, 40; father-son relationship 3–4,
    32–35, 48; *The Interpretation of Dreams*
    9, 71; and Jung 45–46; *Moses and
    Monotheism* 59; nannie 14, 30–31;
    overaffectionate feelings for daughter
    12; *The Psychopathology of Everyday
    Life* 32; siblings 26–27, 32–35; *Three
    Essays on Sexuality* 85; *Totem and Taboo*
    39–40, 57; and unconscious 71–78; in
    Vienna 26–27; Vienna Psychoanalytic
    Society 42–49

Gaylin, W. 17
Gay, P. 17, 26, 93
Gould, S. J. 55
Graf, M. 46, 47
Greenberg, J. 88
Greenberg, R. 88
grievance 93–94
guilt 11–12, 17

Handlbauer, B. 44
Heller, J. B. 29
heredity 4, 40, 95, 97
heresy 3, 47–48, 67
heterosexuality 102–103
Holt, R. 16
Homo sapiens 73, 75
homosexuality 44, 98–99, 103
humanity 2, 26, 74–78
human mental structure 4–5, 77
hysteria 2, 24; Freud's self-diagnosis of 12

"the id" 72
identification 90–91, 105
incest 58, 102

internal conflicts 3, 6; and guilt 12
The Interpretation of Dreams (Freud)
    9, 71

Jung, C.G. 45

Kardiner, A. 17, 19
Kitcher, P. 15, 24, 64
Krull, M. 29

Lachmana, F. 68
Lamarck, J-B. 59, 66
Laplanche J. 88
libido 67, 72, 82
Lieberman, E. J. 47
Loewald, H. 17
Lotto, D. 69
love, psychology of 5, 78–86

MacIntyre, A. 64
Makari, G. 66–67
material reality 13, 17, 78
McGrath, W. 48
Medawar, P. B. 64
Montaigne, M. de 3, 10
Moses and Monotheism (Freud) 59
mother-child relationship 80–81, 89
mother-son relationship, 91–93; *see also*
    Oedipus complex

Napoleon 94–95, 98–99
neurosis 2, 25, 55
nourishments 80–81, 89
Nuremberg Conference 46, 47, 66

obedience, to paternal authority 40, 42
object choice 80–81, 90–91, 93
Oedipus complex 2, 5, 24, 33–34, 88; in
    adolescence and adulthood 102–103;
    cycle of 41; dissolution 96–99; elements
    of 31; family romance 25–32; fathers
    and brothers 32–35; female phallic stage
    99–102; formulation 14–16; foundation
    of 59–60; girl 82; inner struggles 85;
    phallic stage 92–96, 102; pre-Oedipal
    period 89–92, 101; triangular 35, 82
Oedipus Rex (Sophocles) 14, 31
ontogenetic dissolution 96, 98–99

parental/paternal: abuse 20; authority 2,
    38–42; etiology thesis 12
parental perversion, 14–16; *see also* Freud,
    and fathers struggles
parricide 58

phallic stage 92–96, 102
philia 83, 84
phylogenetic inheritance 4, 40, 56–61, 95, 97, 104
Platt, G. 38
Polanyi, M. 63
Pontalis, J. B. 88
Popper, K. 63
preconscious 71
pre-Oedipus period 89–92, 101
primal horde 57, 59
primal phantasy 57, 95
psychic reality 3, 12, 20, 42, 74
psychoanalysis: biology and experience 4; paternal etiology thesis 12
psychoanalysis, and science 3; experts about 63–64; Freud 64–68; post-Freudian 68–69
psychoanalytic psyche 56–59
psychological divisions 4, 6, 9, 18
psychological trauma, of wars 3, 18–19
The Psychopathology of Everyday Life (Freud) 32
puberty 85, 102, 104

Rank, O. 42, 48
reality: fantasy and 17–18; principle 5, 73–74
rebellion 39–40
Recollecting Freud (Sadger) 43, 45
Reik, T. 46–47
repression 77
rivalry 82, 86
romance 78, 84; in adult life 103; in literature 83
Rosensweig, S. 65
Ross, J. M. 15
Rudnytsky, P. 1, 21

Sachs, H. 46
Sadger, I. 43, 48; *Recollecting Freud* 43, 45
Sander, L. 68
Schore, A.: *The Development of the Unconscious Mind* 68
seduction theory 2, 12, 15, 17
self-deception 3, 21
sex/sexual: abuse 2, 3, 13–14, 19–21; disposition 98, 104; identity 80–82; intercourse 83–85; and romance *see* love, psychology of
Shengold, L. 48

siblings 5, 26–27, 32–35, 96
Simon, B. 88
Singer, I. 84
Smith, R. 59
social psychology 4, 9
Solms, M. 68
Sophocles 14; *Oedipus Rex* 14, 31
Sprengnether, M. 32
Stekel, W. 46, 47
Stern, D. 68
Stoycheva, V.: *The Unconscious: Theory, Research, and Clinical Implications* 68–69
subconscious 71, 72
sublimation 5, 74–77
Sulloway, F. 55
super-ego 39, 41, 72, 89, 100

Tallis, F. 16
Thanatos 77
thinking process 73–74, 76
Three Essays on Sexuality (Freud) 85
topographic model 71–72
Totem and Taboo (Freud) 39–40, 57
Tronick, E. 68

unconscious 2, 13–14, 68, 71
The Unconscious: Theory, Research, and Clinical Implications (Weinberger and Stoycheva) 68–69

Vienna Freuds 26–28, 32, 74
Vienna Psychoanalytic Society 3, 42–49
Vinci, L. da 94

Wallerstein, R. 64, 69
war trauma 3, 18–19
Weinberger, J.: *The Unconscious: Theory, Research, and Clinical Implications* 68–69
Weinstein, F. 38
Weltanschauung 64
wet nurse 60, 90, 95
Whitebook, J. 17
Williams, D. C. 63
Wistrich, R. 29
Wittels, F. 44, 46, 47
Wolff, L. 15, 20
Wortis, J. 59

Zepf, S. 15
Zimring, C. 67

For Product Safety Concerns and Information please contact our EU
representative GPSR@taylorandfrancis.com
Taylor & Francis Verlag GmbH, Kaufingerstraße 24, 80331 München, Germany